MONOGRAPHS OF THE
SOCIETY FOR RESEARCH IN
CHILD DEVELOPMENT

Serial No. 241, Vol. 59, No. 4, 1994

THE NATURE AND PROCESSES OF PREVERBAL LEARNING: IMPLICATIONS FROM NINE-MONTH-OLD INFANTS' DISCRIMINATION PROBLEM SOLVING

Jeffrey T. Coldren
John Colombo

WITH COMMENTARY BY
Barry Gholson

AND A REPLY BY THE AUTHORS

Dedicated respectfully to the memory of Jay D. Atwater

MONOGRAPHS OF THE SOCIETY FOR RESEARCH IN CHILD DEVELOPMENT
Serial No. 241, Vol. 59, No. 4, 1994

CONTENTS

ABSTRACT

CoLDREN, JEFFREY T., and COLOMBO, JOHN. The Nature and Processes of
Preverbal Learning: Implications from Nine-Month-Old Infants' Discrimination Problem Solving. With Commentary by BARRY GHOLSON;
and a Reply by JEFFREY T. COLDREN and JOHN COLOMBO. *Monographs
of the Society for Research in Child Development,* 1994, **59**(4, Serial No.
241).

Nine-month-old infants' performance on discrimination-learning problems was investigated in four experiments using the synchronous reinforcement paradigm. These experiments were organized around basic theoretical postulates concerning the relation between attention and learning. In
each of the experiments, infants were trained to respond differentially to
a particular stimulus feature, with the goal of establishing whether they
could learn to respond to a particular stimulus feature under conditions
where other stimulus dimensions were present and varying.

In the first experiment, 48 infants were trained to fixate visually on a
particular feature in a pair of stimuli that varied in color, form, and position
dimensions. Contingencies for responding were then shifted either within
a dimension (reversal shift) or across dimensions (nonreversal shift). Infants
learned to respond to the reinforced feature during initial training; moreover, infants assigned to a reversal shift condition showed a higher level of
transfer of learning during the test phase than those assigned to a nonreversal shift condition.

The second experiment extended the results of Experiment 1 by testing
48 additional infants under conditions in which the number of varying
irrelevant dimensions was increased during the shift phase. Although the
difficulty added to this task by this manipulation made transfer more difficult for all infants, results again indicated that transfer of learning was more
evident for infants in a reversal shift than a nonreversal shift condition.

In the third experiment, 64 infants were trained in a similar manner,
except that completely new values were substituted during shift phases on

the color and form dimensions. This manipulation was meant to probe whether infants were formulating a dimension response from previous training and to test the predictions of such dimension processing for transfer of learning to a functionally new problem. Infants were reinforced for fixating on a new feature either within the same dimension as during training (intradimension shift) or within the dimension that was not originally trained (extradimension shift). Transfer of learning was clearly superior in the intradimension shift condition.

The findings of the first three experiments suggested that, during discrimination-learning problems, infants selected and tested individual stimulus features and dimensions from an array of potential solutions to the problem until discovering the one that was consistently associated with reinforcement. To explore this possibility further in a fourth experiment, 28 infants were trained to fixate on a stimulus compound until reaching a learning criterion. This was done to determine whether backward learning curves plotted from the data might be discontinuous (i.e., show a step-like increase from chance levels to criterion levels at the attainment of the solution), which would be consistent with the inference that infants were selecting among dimensions in solving this task. Backward learning curves were indeed discontinuous; presolution levels hovered at chance, and a precipitous rise was observed at the point of solution. Furthermore, a postlearning probe that dissociated the compound features on which infants were trained showed a dominance of color over form. Individual infants who showed this particular dominance solved the learning task faster than those who did not, further suggesting that responding based on the selection of particular dimensions of stimuli facilitated learning.

The results of these experiments indicate that infants can learn complex discriminations under conditions in which stimuli vary in up to three dimensions; such performance implies the ability to attend to differentiated stimulus features. The results also provide strong evidence that, by 9 months of age, infants process such compound stimuli in a dimensional manner; that is, in addition to being able to parse individual stimulus features from the whole, infants are aware that particular features comprise separable dimensions and can base their responding on those dimensions. The finding of such dimension processing in preverbal humans indicates that major revisions are necessary in interpretations that have been held for nearly 30 years concerning developmental changes in children's discrimination learning. Finally, and perhaps most important, the present studies strongly suggest that infants learn and solve discrimination-learning problems in a manner that involves the categorical selection and testing of features from the environment.

I. INTRODUCTION

The discovery in the late 1950s that human infants display tendencies to fixate on stimuli preferentially had at least two important consequences for the study of early development (Berlyne, 1958; Fantz, 1958, 1964). First, these findings challenged long-held notions that infants were merely passive recipients of environmental experience; instead, they suggested that, from birth, humans actively choose aspects of the environment toward which to direct their attention (Fantz, 1961; McCall, 1975; Stone, Smith, & Murphy, 1973). Second, Fantz's finding was the basis for the development of techniques to study preverbal perceptual-cognitive functioning that capitalized on infants' fixation tendencies. Through the use of these techniques, such as the habituation and paired-comparison procedures, research in this area has flourished, documenting a range of relatively sophisticated perceptual, discrimination, attention, and learning abilities in early life (see the reviews in Banks & Salapatek, 1983; Cohen & Salapatek, 1975; Olson & Sherman, 1983; Rovee-Collier, 1987).

Despite advances in verifying infants' ability to process environmental input, this literature has been criticized for being static and product oriented (Haith, 1990; Sophian, 1980). Its primary theme during the 1960s and 1970s was the cataloging of infants' perceptual-attention and learning abilities (see Horowitz & Colombo, 1990), an emphasis similar to that seen during the period of normative research in developmental psychology that spanned the 1930s, 1940s, and 1950s (Sears, 1975; Stevenson, 1983).

For example, convincing evidence exists that infants can discriminate among individual components of stimuli in terms of color and form (Cohen, 1973; Cohen & Gelber, 1975; Cohen, Gelber, & Lazar, 1971; Colombo, McCollam, Coldren, Mitchell, & Rash, 1990). From evidence indicating that infants have recognition memory skills (Fagan & McGrath, 1981; Rose & Feldman, 1990) and show stimulus categorization or classification (Colombo, O'Brien, Mitchell, Roberts, & Horowitz, 1987; Younger, 1990; Younger & Cohen, 1986), it is clear that infants represent these properties of stimuli cognitively. Further, it has long been known that infants can be conditioned

1

and can retain learned responses across long intervals at early ages (Rovee & Rovee, 1969; Rovee-Collier, 1987). While the accumulation of data on the behavioral capacities of infants was impressive and valuable for advancing information about infants' competence, it has provided only a partial portrait of cognitive functioning, with an emphasis on what infants were capable of. That is, this work focused on the *products* of early cognitive abilities.

What has not been made readily available from this line of inquiry is knowledge of how infants actually use such capacities during the performance of tasks, such as acquiring information or solving a problem. Investigators working with older children have argued that research needs to move beyond merely describing states of knowledge and instead attempt to determine how these states of knowledge are acquired (Glaser, 1981, 1990; Greeno, 1980; Stevenson, 1983). By focusing on *how* a task is approached, one may observe and document the *process* by which such cognitive products are attained (Brown, 1982; Linder & Siegel, 1983; Mitchell, 1988; Siegler, 1983; Underwood, 1975). Thus, although much may be known about the end products of cognitive processes in infants, the central focus of the proposed approach is understanding how cognitive processes are involved and operate in the acquisition or achievement of an end response (Gholson & Beilin, 1979).

This more dynamic approach offers a specific strategy for studying how infants' attention abilities are deployed in the course of attaining a goal, performing a task, or solving a problem. To go beyond the level of demonstrating the existence of abilities in preverbal humans, information is needed on how cognitive processes actually perform and interact when called on to reach a particular end. Specifically, data are needed to determine how infants are able to select visually among several features of stimuli when other features are present and varying, particularly when only one of the features is relevant for solving a problem or performing a task. Furthermore, it is virtually unknown how infants direct and redirect their attention to critical stimulus features and whether such selection changes over trials as a function of experience (e.g., Broadbent, 1971; Neill, 1977; Well, Lorch, & Anderson, 1980). Another related issue concerns whether attention would be directed toward features or toward the higher-order dimensions that these features exemplify and whether such attention could be used to allow some advantage in another, similar problem that requires selective attention (e.g., Brown, 1982; Holland, Holyoak, Nisbett, & Thagard, 1986).

The issues of infants' capacities for discrimination and attention and of their deployment of these capacities during task performance are important because of the critical role that these mental processes play in an infant's everyday functioning (e.g., Boff, Kaufman, & Thomas, 1986). From a range of impinging and varying stimuli, the infant must find the particular stimulus event that is relevant for solving the task at hand in the face of other competing and simultaneously occurring events (e.g., Broadbent, 1958; Enns & Cameron, 1987; Lane & Pearson, 1982; Navon & Gopher, 1979; Treisman, 1986). Thus, it is necessary that the infant's limited attention resources be focused on the most critical and informative portions of the stimulus quickly and efficiently.

DISCRIMINATION LEARNING

To address these issues in infants, we first turned to studies of discrimination learning in children and adults. The discrimination-learning paradigm has remained a significant force throughout the field of experimental child psychology since the 1930s. And, over the years, the central issue to which this paradigm has been applied has been the investigation of the processes by which subjects respond to stimuli in order to reach a solution to a problem.

One of the reasons for the continuing influence of this issue has been the depth and adaptability of the theoretical explanations that have been put forth to account for the process of discrimination learning. In its inception, the experimental literature on this topic was inclined to propose explanations of children's solutions that were based on then-dominant theories of conditioning and learning. Later, as cognitive theory was embraced by the field during the 1960s and 1970s, theories of discrimination learning were generally revised to include propositions that specified children as engaging in active selection and testing of responses to reach the solution to a problem. Clearly, many of the issues surrounding the processes of discrimination learning and problem solving are still prevalent today, as may be seen in recent investigations reported by Gholson (Gholson, Dattell, Morgan, & Eymard, 1989; Gholson & Rosenthal, 1984).

Another reason that the study of discrimination learning has been so prominent is its empirical rigor. The paradigm offers a specific and quantitative approach as well as an experimental task to determine the manner in which processes such as stimulus perception, selective attention, and representation operate during information acquisition and problem solving.

For these reasons, this literature on older subjects seemed ideal as a series of guidelines for our investigative goals with infants.

PURPOSE AND PLAN

The purpose of this *Monograph* is to investigate the relation between perceptual-attention processes and their functioning in tasks that involve the active acquisition of information in reaching the solution to a problem. As such, the goal is not merely to document that attention processes operate in these tasks but rather to observe *how* they operate in guiding attention in dynamic situations.

In what follows, we first provide in Chapter II a general overview of the theoretical issues in the discrimination-learning literature and of the empirical tests that have been made of those issues. The original theoretical positions regarding the nature of discrimination learning are introduced in this chapter, and we discuss how these positions have been adapted to the study of children with particular emphasis on the mechanisms that have been posited to account for developmental changes in discrimination-learning performance; the models are presented in their historical context so as to convey how the theoretical positions have changed throughout the years. Finally, the theoretical implications of the discrimination-learning models for the performance of infants on such tasks is explicated, and extant data from the infancy literature pertinent to these issues are reviewed.

In the following two chapters we describe four experiments in which hypotheses concerning infants' performance in discrimination-learning tasks were tested. The basic aim of the first two experiments (Chap. III) was to test fundamental predictions concerning the necessity of verbal processes for infants' discrimination-learning performance. The purpose of the third and fourth experiments (Chap. IV) was to determine the nature of infants' representation and of the processes guiding attention selection in these tasks.

The *Monograph* concludes with a discussion of the significance that the results of these four experiments have for understanding infants' acquisition of information, illuminating the nature and processes of discrimination learning, and extending and revising the developmental and theoretical implications of discrimination learning.

II. THEORETICAL AND EMPIRICAL ISSUES
IN THE STUDY OF DISCRIMINATION LEARNING

In the typical discrimination-learning task, the subject is simultaneously presented with two visual stimuli, one to the left and one to the right of midline. The stimulus pairs usually consist of chromatic geometric forms that can be described in terms of broad classes of features—called *dimensions*—that share a common property such as form, color, brightness, or size (Zeaman & House, 1963). Each of these dimensions is composed of specific individual values, which have been referred to as *attributes, cues,* or *features;* for the sake of consistency, the term *feature* will be used throughout this *Monograph* to refer to an individual cue on a dimension. Thus, for instance, a particular discrimination-learning problem may contain the dimensions of color, form, and position, each of which contains, respectively, the features of green and blue, triangle and circle, and left and right. A response (e.g., choosing, touching, labeling) to one of these stimuli (which is arbitrarily chosen) is then rewarded, while a response to the other stimulus of the pair is not.

In the simplest form of the task, the two stimuli are identical, varying only in their spatial position relative to the subject. Thus, only one dimension (position) is differentially rewarded, and the subject must learn the discrimination on the basis of left versus right. In more complex forms of the task, the stimuli may vary on additional dimensions; for example, in a two-dimensional task, the stimuli may vary in color (e.g., red vs. blue) as well as position. Here, the subject's task is to learn to respond on the basis of any one of four possible features; if the correct feature is red, the subject must respond to this feature by focusing on the color dimension, regardless of variation in the position dimension (or vice versa). In a three-dimensional task (which is the most common configuration), form is also varied, and now the subject must be able to discover (and respond on the basis of) the correct feature while ignoring variation in two other, irrelevant dimensions.

DISCONTINUITY VERSUS CONTINUITY IN THE PROCESS
OF DISCRIMINATION LEARNING

The literature on discrimination learning originated from two basic and conflicting accounts of how subjects solve such tasks (see Trabasso & Bower, 1968). The first position proposed that the subject sequentially attends to, and tests, different stimulus features that might lead to a successful solution of the problem at hand (Krechevsky, 1932a, 1932b, 1933, 1938; Lashley, 1929). If the selected feature is not reinforced, the subject learns only that the current choice is incorrect (Bower & Trabasso, 1964; Krechevsky, 1938; Trabasso & Bower, 1968). Eventually, the subject does choose the correct feature and is rewarded—and the problem is solved. As a result of this sequence, the correct response is not made until just before solution and thus yields a learning curve termed *discontinuous* that contains a single, steep upward step (Krechevsky, 1938). The subject's selection and testing of any single feature during the learning sequence was termed a *hypothesis* (e.g., Gholson, 1980; Krechevsky, 1932a; Levine, 1975).

In contrast to this model of attention selection, Spence argued that subjects perceived *all* reinforced features in stimulus compounds, that habit strength to all these accrued, and that, by virtue of being reinforced most often, the feature that yielded the correct solution to the discrimination-learning problem gradually accumulated greater excitatory or positive response strength (Spence, 1936, 1937b, 1960). Concurrently, subjects' choice of incorrect features increased inhibitory or negative response strength. The accumulation of response strength over trials yielded a learning curve that was *continuous* in nature (Spence, 1938, 1940).

DEVELOPMENTAL STUDIES OF DISCRIMINATION LEARNING

These early positions espoused by Krechevsky and Spence had a major influence on the development of models of children's discrimination learning. One set of models used by researchers seeking to investigate the discrimination-learning performance of children developed directly out of Spence's model of continuous conditioning, and another set was based on the application of the notion of hypothesis testing to children. Both sets of models are reviewed in the following sections.

Conditioning-based Theories

Verbal Mediation Theory

The Kendlers specifically set out to test the applicability of Spence's (1936) continuity model with subjects across a wide developmental range

(Kendler & Kendler, 1962; Kendler, 1983). While Spence's predictions generally held for young subjects (younger than approximately 5 years), they were found *not* to apply to older children and college-aged students (Kendler & Kendler, 1962). A mechanism called *mediation,* in which some property or dimension of the stimulus was internally represented and used to direct the response, was posited to account for this difference in discrimination learning between younger and older children (e.g., Kendler, Glucksberg, & Keston, 1961). Mediation was conceptualized as an intervening step in the learning process that was most likely verbal in nature and that should therefore be unavailable to preverbal subjects (Kendler, Glasman, & Ward, 1972; Kendler & Kendler, 1968; Kendler, 1963, 1972; Spence, 1937a). As a result of this mediation deficiency, the performance of very young children on such tasks was proposed to take place according to the buildup and extinction of excitatory strength as predicted from Spence's (1936) theory.

The Kendlers' theory, then, posited a basic developmental change in a process underlying the relation between attention and learning (Amsel, 1989). The proposed developmental transitions in learning were examined by using a methodology that employed different types of *shifts* in reinforcement after standard training on basic two- or three-dimensional discrimination-learning tasks had been given. In these shift paradigms, subjects were trained in a three-dimensional (color, form, position) discrimination-learning problem and then assigned to one of two groups that received an additional experimental phase in which the same stimuli were presented but the basis of reinforcement was changed (Buss, 1953; Kendler & Kendler, 1975; see also Fig. 1). Essentially, the purpose of this manipulation was to determine whether the relevant feature or dimension that the subject extracted during initial training was transferred to the functionally new problem.

Reversal and nonreversal shift tasks.—Two types of shifts were employed in this paradigm. In a *reversal* (R) shift, the experimenter trained the child to respond to a particular feature of a dimension (e.g., the color blue) and then switched reinforcement contingencies to the other feature within the same dimension (e.g., the color green). In a *nonreversal* (NR) shift, the reinforcement was switched from a feature in one dimension to a feature in another one (e.g., from the color blue to the form of a triangle or circle).

According to Spence's theory, evidence for transfer should be more readily observed in NR shifts than in R shifts (Kendler & D'Amato, 1955; Kendler & Kendler, 1962; Kendler, 1960). This was predicted because response strength accrued to the previously incorrect feature within the same dimension (here, the color green) would be uniformly inhibitory whereas the response strength to stimulus features in the other dimension (i.e., either of the forms) was neutral.

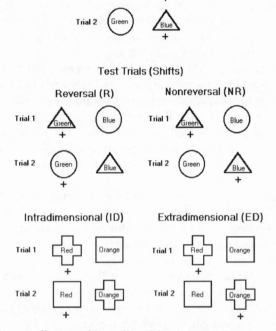

FIG. 1.—Two paradigms used in studies of discrimination learning: the reversal (R)/nonreversal (NR) and intradimension (ID)/extradimension (ED) shift tasks. The reinforced stimulus is indicated by a plus sign.

Conversely, under the assumption of a verbal mediator, a higher level of transfer from initial training would be expected to occur in R than in NR shift conditions because the mediator would facilitate selection of (or attention to) the relevant dimension (e.g., color or form) rather than to individual specifics (i.e., blue/green or circle/square) of the stimulus array. If during initial discrimination training the subject is basing a response on a particular dimension, then the fact that the same dimension remains relevant in an R shift would lead to an easier transferral to the new feature within that dimension when reinforcement is shifted. In the NR shift, however, focus on a particular dimension would lead to more incorrect choices, as the subject now must formulate a response to a dimension that had been previously irrelevant (Kendler & Kendler, 1962).

Developmental findings.—Using these paradigms, the prediction of a developmental transition in how children solved discrimination-learning problems was confirmed. Preschool children solved NR shifts more rapidly than

R shifts, and children older than 5 years solved the R shift more rapidly than the NR shift (Kendler et al., 1972; Kendler & Kendler, 1968; Kendler, 1972, 1974; Kendler, Kendler, & Learnard, 1962; Kendler, Kendler, & Wells, 1960). Thus, children younger than approximately 5 years of age appeared to learn incrementally and nonselectively, just as Spence's (1936) model predicted, while mediated responding emerged at later ages (Kendler & Kendler, 1962; Kendler, 1979a, 1983). However, kindergarten children found R and NR shifts equally difficult, leading to the conclusion that, at intermediate ages, there were individual differences in the use of mediators (Kendler & Kendler, 1959).

Differentiation Theory

At approximately the same time that the Kendlers' mediation model was actively being tested, another model of discrimination learning in children that also received a great deal of attention from investigators was proposed. However, in contrast to the emphasis placed by the mediation model on the child's activities of modifying or supplementing stimulus input through association or selection, the Tighes' alternative conceptualization emphasized the subject's sensitivity to stimulus input (Tighe & Tighe, 1966). Following the tenets of perceptual learning theory, this model stressed the important role of perceptual processes that were necessary to solve a discrimination problem. Discrimination learning occurred through differentiation, which may be defined as an increasing sensitivity to existing but initially undetected properties of the stimuli (e.g., Gibson & Gibson, 1955; Tighe & Tighe, 1966). That is, subjects must distinguish among the dimensions that are present in the stimulus array, and only when this is accomplished are they able to learn the stimulus-reward (S-R) relations required to solve the discrimination problem.

Since the postulated process initially involves learning to perceive the component dimensions, investigators tested predictions that follow from the differentiation model regarding the beneficial effect of perceptual experience using the R/NR shift tasks. In the R shift, the same dimension is relevant across the training and test phases. However, in an NR shift—in which another dimension is now relevant—further perceptual differentiation may be necessary to enable responding to the newly relevant dimension. Hence, experience with the stimuli that promoted perceptual differentiation of the dimensions was predicted to help R shift performance. Five- to six-year-olds were given perceptual pretraining experience in distinguishing the relevant dimension prior to the actual discrimination-learning task; as was predicted, these children performed R shifts easier than NR shifts (Tighe, 1965; Tighe & Tighe, 1969). The finding was also supported by developmental data; 10-year-olds, who were presumably more perceptually experienced with objects, responded to stimuli in terms of their dimensions, whereas 4-year-olds, who had presumably less perceptual experience, treated stimulus pairs as independent and unrelated (Cole, 1973; Tighe, 1973; Tighe, Glick, & Cole, 1971; Tighe & Tighe, 1967).

The implications of this model contrasted with those implications of Spence's theory, in which differentiated perception of individual stimulus features was presumed to be present at the outset of discrimination training. It also contrasted with the Kendlers' proposition that, beyond perceptual differentiation, verbal mediation was necessary to control learning; the Tighes argued that verbalization was superfluous.

Attention Theory

Like the Kendlers' model, the attention theory of Zeaman and House (1963, 1979) also reflected the influence of Spence's theorizing. These authors based their model on Spence's (1936, 1940) notion that an important part of learning to make a discrimination involves the orienting of sensory receptors to the discriminative features (see also Wyckoff, 1952). Zeaman and House (1963) extended the concept of the orienting response from reflecting a simple physical response to the presented stimuli (e.g., visual fixation, head turn) to a more covert, selective attention response to the various dimensions of the stimuli with which reinforcement might be associated. If the subject had difficulty making such an *orienting response* (OR) to the stimuli involved, discrimination learning obviously would be commensurately slowed. Thus, unlike the Kendlers' theory, Zeaman and House's (1963) model did not posit a verbal mediation influence but instead asserted that an attention response was necessary in order to solve a discrimination-learning problem.

Support for these investigators' position was found in their studies of learning by subjects with Down syndrome (House & Zeaman, 1960). Zeaman and House (1963) adopted Hayes's (1953) procedure of plotting learning curves *backward* from the learning criterion in such a way that every subject's data are aligned on the last point prior to attaining the criterion. The resulting backward curves that they obtained typically consisted of a period of presolution trial performance at chance levels followed by a sudden and steep rise at criterion. The authors interpreted the early, flat portion of the curve as a period during which the subject was either not attending to any stimulus property (i.e., an OR was not occurring) or attending to some stimulus property that was irrelevant to the solution of the task (i.e., an OR was occurring but was incorrectly directed).

This reasoning was expressed in a formal model that specified the OR as a centrally based attention response that was directed to stimulus dimensions. The dimension selected by the subject may be either relevant or irrelevant to solving the discrimination problem; whichever the case, features on that dimension are then exposed. Thus, for example, if the subject directs attention to the color dimension, green and blue features are revealed. Immediately following the initial OR, an instrumental response occurs to one of the features in that dimension. Thus, if color is the relevant dimension, the subject then makes an instrumental response that associates the positive blue feature with reinforcement. If the subject focused on selects the irrelevant dimension of form, then either one of the two negative features, triangle or circle, will be selected.

Intradimension and extradimension shift tasks.—The predictions of attention theory were tested with another version of the design in which children's performance across two different types of shifts of reinforcement is tested after training on a standard discrimination-learning problem (Shepp & Turrisi, 1966; Wolff, 1967; Zeaman & House, 1963; see also Fig. 1). In an *intradimension* (ID) shift, the experimenter reinforces responding to a novel feature on the same dimension (in Fig. 1, color), whereas, in an *extradimension* (ED) shift, responding to a novel feature on the opposite dimension (in Fig. 1, form) is reinforced. These two shift tasks are similar in rationale and execution to the previously described R and NR shifts; however, they are procedurally different in that new features are used on dimensions during the shift phase of the ID/ED task.

Thus, for instance, while color (or form) remains the relevant dimension in both the training and the shift phases of the ID task, the specific color (or form) used in the shift phase of the task differs from what it was in the training phase. The rationale behind the ID/ED shift task is nevertheless similar to that underlying the R/NR shift; if in solving the task during initial training the subject is making an OR (i.e., selectively attending) to the relevant dimension, that dimension should be more readily recognized and chosen as a basis for responding when reinforcement is shifted to another of its exemplar features. Thus, an OR to the relevant dimension should facilitate learning during the ID shift phase of the task, even though the specific features are completely different (Campione, Hyman, & Zeaman, 1965). Furthermore, dimension learning and transfer of attention to a relevant dimension should be observable in both nonverbal and preverbal organisms.

Developmental findings.—Several investigations supported this prediction of attention theory by finding that preschool and elementary school children, as well as children with mental retardation, learned ID shifts faster than ED shifts (Campione, 1970; Campione et al., 1965; Dickerson, 1966; Eimas, 1966; House & Zeaman, 1962; Mumbauer & Odom, 1967; see also the reviews in Shepp & Turrisi, 1966; Wolff, 1967). Taken together, conver-

gent results obtained with subjects who varied in age and language development supported the proposition that an OR to the relevant dimension of
the stimuli was necessary for the process of learning a discrimination to
occur. Further, this evidence pointed to the role of nonverbal, attention
processes in learning and indicated that the function of the OR in the
process of learning did not appear to undergo any fundamental developmental change (Dickerson, Novik, & Gould, 1972).

A Theoretical Transition in the Models

At the beginning of the 1970s, several reviews of the literature concluded that the attention model gave the most convincing theoretical and
empirical account of children's discrimination learning (Esposito, 1975;
Shepp & Turrisi, 1966; Slamecka, 1968; Wolff, 1967). However, these reviews also contained several criticisms that forced a theoretical reorientation
in the study of discrimination learning.

One criticism focused on the methodological differences in different
applications of the shift task and on the consequent difficulty in drawing
conclusions across studies. Another criticism that emerged was that the differences between the theoretical positions may be more supposed than real
since investigators routinely translated constructs from rival models into
their own frameworks.

Thus, it became apparent that some other model could conceivably
incorporate all the data (Stevenson, 1972; White, 1970). Hunt (1961) argued
that the strength of the methodology underlying discrimination-learning
tasks required extension beyond S-R theory: the neobehavioristic approach
of attempting to maintain parsimony while trying to enlarge the framework
of S-R learning theories was causing conflicts within the camp (White, 1970).
Neobehaviorism no longer represented a cohesive theoretical forefront of
research on children's learning, and the underlying theory behind all discrimination-learning models was in need of change (Stevenson, 1983). Com-
menting on these points, Kendler and Kendler (1975) observed that the
proposed theoretical processes may not, in fact, be incompatible; all the
extant models were incomplete and could benefit from further extension
and refinement, and their further development would not be best served by
focusing on differences. Following these authors' observations, investigators
took a distinctly cognitive view of learning in which, theoretically, all the
processes postulated heretofore could reside without conflict.

Hypothesis-Testing Models

The history of hypothesis-testing models of discrimination learning
evolved from the Lashley/Krechevsky position and followed a path distinct

from that of the conditioning-based models. At the same time that researchers were investigating children's discrimination learning guided by Spence's theory, investigators in the domain of adult discrimination learning had accepted and were employing a hypothesis-testing orientation during the 1950s (Bruner, Goodnow, & Austin, 1956; Estes, 1960; Levine, 1975; Restle, 1960; Rock, 1957). This theoretical position allowed researchers to concentrate on the primary issue that had been raised by Lashley's (1929) initial observations, namely, investigating subjects' *hypotheses* during problem solving through analysis of their response patterns (Levine, 1975). Further, as a result of the acceptance of hypothesis-testing models of discrimination learning in adults, a shift occurred in research with children leading away from the continuity position that had dominated the early literature and toward the discontinuity-of-learning position. This position, which explicitly accepted sequential selection and active testing of responses in children, was formulated in the two models of hypothesis testing to be reviewed next.

Gholson's Cognitive-Developmental Model

Gholson's model specified explicitly the manner in which children selected and tested hypotheses during information acquisition (Gholson, 1980; Gholson & Beilin, 1979). To do so, the pattern of children's responses while solving a discrimination problem was observed; specifically, blank trials—which are simply one or more trials in which the experimenter provides no feedback to the subject—were interspersed systematically among feedback trials (Levine, 1966). These blank trials served as probes to test for the subject's use of a particular hypothesis. The adoption of each hypothesis (e.g., "focus on color") is indicated by a unique pattern of responses by the subject (Levine, 1966, 1975); if the subject shows a pattern of responding that does not correspond to any possible hypothesis, it may be concluded that the subject is responding randomly.

Gholson, Levine, and Phillips (1972) found that kindergartners used hypotheses in less than half of their response patterns. Not surprisingly, position-preference and position-alternation patterns accounted for most of the responses that did not correspond to legitimate hypotheses. Thus, for the youngest children, response sets—which were not sensitive to feedback—dominated responding.

For older children, however, response patterns conforming to the presence of hypotheses dominated the responding of second, fourth, and sixth graders and of college students (Gholson et al., 1972). Further, when backward learning curves were constructed for each age group by aligning data points on the trial of last error (TLE), the resulting curve showed that the percentage of correct responding before the TLE was stationary at around

50%, suggesting that up to this point the subject is correct only by chance. After the TLE, the shape of the learning curve showed a sharp increase in the percentage of correct responding just before reaching the learning criterion, indicating that a subject never made another error after sampling the correct hypothesis (Bower & Trabasso, 1964; Trabasso & Bower, 1968). Thus, elementary school children and college students did not discover the correct hypothesis before the TLE, but they did hold it after that trial.

To account for the prevalence of response sets at the younger ages and of prediction hypotheses at older ages, Gholson et al. (1972) proposed that children use one of two systems to generate hypotheses. The system of strategies involves sequences of hypotheses that eventually lead to correct responding (focusing, dimension checking, hypothesis checking). The other system, that of stereotypes (stimulus preference, position alteration, position preference), never leads to solutions and is insensitive to feedback, even when it involves repeated disconfirmation. Gholson et al. (1972) found that college students and elementary school children predominantly displayed strategies, whereas kindergarten children exhibited mostly stereotype systems, especially position alteration.

Gholson (Gholson, 1980; Gholson & Beilin, 1979) articulated these hypothesis-testing systems in a cognitive-developmental model positing that a child's performance on a discrimination-learning task was a function of two components: a central processor, which serves an executive function to carry out logical operations such as determining the hypothesis system, and various cognitive subprocesses that are responsible for getting information to the processor and include attention, perception, coding, and memory processes. Piaget's theory of structuralism accounted for changes in the operation of the processor, and the development of information-processing capacities explained changes in the efficiency of the necessary cognitive subcomponents. Thus, Gholson's (1980) model conceptualized developmental change in solving discrimination problems both in qualitative and in quantitative terms.

T. S. Kendler's Level-of-Functioning Model

In response to severe criticisms of the earlier mediation model (e.g., Esposito, 1975; Shepp & Turrisi, 1966; Slamecka, 1968; Wolff, 1967) as well as the influx of hypothesis-testing theories (e.g., Gholson & Beilin, 1979), T. S. Kendler (1979a, 1983) revised her earlier account of children's discrimination learning. This new version posited a developmental progression in the predominant mode in which children solve discrimination-learning problems. Nonselective and parallel encoding of features of stimuli was proposed to characterize functioning in the lower level (mode). Following Spence's (1936) model, response strength to the correct feature is considered to increase in increments as a function of reinforcement, while the decrease in response strength inhibits responding to nonreinforced features. The accumulated strength to the reinforced component directly determines the probability of choosing the correct stimulus. At the higher level of functioning, encoding occurs selectively, and problem solving occurs through the selection and testing of hypotheses.

The mode in which discrimination-learning problems are solved depends on the functioning of behavior-regulation (hypothesis-testing) and information-processing (encoding) components. Unlike the earlier model (Kendler & Kendler, 1968; Kendler, 1963), Kendler's revised model did not posit verbal mediation as being responsible for developmental differences in discrimination learning. Instead, this model relied on differences in the maturation of levels in the central neural system (CNS) as the mechanism underlying differences in levels of encoding and problem solving (Kendler, 1979a; Rust & Kendler, 1987). The lower CNS levels associated with nonselective encoding and incremental learning mature earlier than the higher levels that are required for selective encoding and hypothesis testing. Despite this difference in proposed mechanisms, the fundamental nature of the theory appears not to have changed in that it still posited a basic developmental change in the type of process underlying learning.

In validating the levels-of-functioning theory, T. S. Kendler (1979a, 1983) found that the mode in which subjects encoded and solved problems varied with developmental level; children younger than approximately 5 years operated in the lower mode of nonselective encoding and incremental learning, as demonstrated by their better performance on nonreversal than on reversal shifts. Children older than 5 years appeared to function in the higher mode of selective attention and hypothesis testing, revealed by their application of a win-stay rule to the problem (i.e., selecting the stimulus just reinforced).

FURTHER DIRECTIONS FOR THE STUDY OF DISCRIMINATION LEARNING

As should be evident from the preceding review, the longevity of interest in issues surrounding the theory and method of discrimination learning has led to an evolution of both the questions asked within the paradigm and the theoretical interpretations of the findings. This interest has not abated: there have been recent calls for studies that would amend previously established understanding of the processes involved in discrimination learning with newly emergent concepts and empirical findings from the cognitive and information-processing frameworks (House, 1989; Siegler, 1983) since these theoretical approaches share the common goal of identifying processes by which subjects select and represent stimuli during the process of learning (Spiker & Cantor, 1983). In fact, it has even been suggested that the study of learning was already being explored in recent years under the thinly disguised rubric of cognitive psychology: "The time has come to return to the study of all types of learning in children. In part, this is a call to return to unfinished business, but perhaps just as important is the need to integrate existing information on learning with important new findings in cognitive development" (Cantor & Spiker, 1989, p. 123).

Indeed, the discrimination-learning literature is being currently expanded by investigations of children's analogical reasoning (Gholson et al., 1989). The analogical-reasoning approach represents a logical extension of the hypothesis-testing models in that it explores children's transfer of abstract concepts and sequential operations across various stimulus dimensions. As such, it demonstrates the applicability of such models to complex and higher-order learning abilities that are currently under study within the cognitive framework.

While Gholson et al.'s (1989) recent work represents an extension of these models to more complex behavior (e.g., Gholson & Rosenthal, 1984), a second branch of the discrimination-learning literature that extends in the opposite direction has been largely overlooked. This extension, which involves the application of the discrimination-learning paradigm and theoretical models to what might be characterized as simpler organisms, namely, preverbal infants, is the focus of the present *Monograph*. The implications of this research for the study of both the phenomenon of discrimination learning and the human infant are detailed below.

Implications of Infant Studies

While the study of discrimination learning dominated the literature of experimental child psychology for 30 years, investigators have largely left the infants' performance on such tasks unconsidered, both theoretically and empirically. Given that the study of discrimination learning has involved a wide developmental and phylogenetic range, the omission of infants is conspicuous. Although the exact reason for this exclusion has never been made clear, one very likely cause is that during the 1960s—the time when investigators were testing models of discrimination learning with children—the scientific study of infancy was just newly emerging in terms of both theory and, perhaps more important, technology.

In fact, Caron and Caron (1978) pointed out some time ago that the study of discrimination learning represented a potentially fruitful avenue for gaining access to cognitive functioning in preverbal organisms, particularly as it concerns the interrelation between attention and learning. Testing how infants attend to and select a particular stimulus feature under conditions in which other stimulus features are present and varying is clearly relevant in advancing such understanding. Furthermore, it is also important to determine the developmental course of the relation between attention and learning processes in preverbal infants of different ages; such data should reveal the nature and origins of more mature abilities and hence begin to close the gap in our understanding of how cognitive processes emerge out of infancy and into childhood (Haith, 1990; Siegler, 1983).

In addition to advancing understanding of issues related to the development of preverbal cognitive functions, inclusion of infants in investigations of theoretical models of discrimination learning has a unique potential for settling long-standing and as yet unresolved debates over its nature and processes (e.g., Kendler, 1983; Rust & Kendler, 1987). As noted earlier, the literature contains two views that are at odds over whether a transition occurs in the learning processes of children.

The Kendlers' formula holds that, whereas the performance of young children suggests a gradual, cumulative process that is consistent with Spence's (1936) account of continuous accretion of response strengths as a function of previous reinforcements, learning in older children and adults is more consistent with Krechevsky's (1932b) notion of discontinuous (i.e., all-or-none) learning, which connotes selection and testing of responses in the course of solution (Kendler, 1979a). The emergence of a verbal system is posited to be responsible for this qualitative transition; such a system would facilitate the capacity to extract and verbally label a dimension and thereby aid in the formulation of a systematic set of responses to be tested (Kendler & Kendler, 1962).

An opposing theoretical account offered by Zeaman and House (1963) maintains that an orienting response functions to direct attention to the dimension that is relevant for solving the discrimination problem and that the critical point in complex learning and problem solving is the isolation of the relevant dimension. Since according to this account such isolation may be accomplished through simple orienting, the role of verbal processes and developmental transitions in discrimination learning is seriously challenged.

These points of contention between attention theory and the Kendlers' mediation model remain unresolved to this day (Gholson & Schuepfer, 1979; Kendler, 1979b; Rust & Kendler, 1987; Tighe & Tighe, 1987). Most interestingly, the two views make diametrically opposed predictions for how infants should perform on a discrimination task; hence, infant research can yield critical information concerning the relative import of verbal mediation and of attention in subjects who are intact (i.e., not cognitively delayed) and preverbal. Additionally, findings in this domain can also have important practical consequences for work aimed at assisting infants and children with developmental, attention, learning, or cognitive disabilities associate relevant portions of the stimulus environment with their consequences (Barkley, 1989; Bickel, Stella, & Etzel, 1984; Schreibman, 1975).

Research on Cognitive Processes during Learning in Infancy

Unfortunately, there is little in the literature on infant learning that is directly relevant to understanding the interrelation between attention and the solving of discrimination-learning problems. One reason for this lack is that, in past decades, investigators of infant learning typically focused on simpler or more basic questions, such as whether the infant was conditionable and, if so, at what age this might be first documented.

During the 1950s and 1960s, when the development and testing of discrimination-learning models in children was at its peak, developmental psychologists were just beginning to explore the operant and classical learning capacities of infants (e.g., Horowitz, 1968; Kessen, 1963; Lipsitt, 1966; Stevenson, 1970). In the course of their efforts, these investigators also collected extensive data on infants' abilities to be differentially conditioned to various stimuli, including color (Lipsitt, 1963; Simmons, 1964; Simmons & Lipsitt, 1961), color and form (Weisberg & Simmons, 1966), lateral position (Siqueland, 1964; Siqueland & Lipsitt, 1966), size (Graham, Ernhart, Craft, & Berman, 1964; Hill, 1965), sound (Papousek, 1967), and depth (Bower, 1964). However, despite the wealth of the data that were collected, the theoretical scope of this literature was limited largely to the more fundamental issues, such as documenting whether infants were capable of discriminations in learning procedures (e.g., see Fagen & Ohr, 1990).

Twenty-five years ago, Horowitz (1968) challenged developmental psychologists to reach beyond the simple demonstration of infant capabilities and work toward identifying the mechanisms underpinning behavioral change across the life span. Unfortunately, this bid went largely unheeded, and the potential for the study of learning per se in infancy was never fully realized.

Although research on the processes underlying infant learning has received little attention, research *involving* infant learning has in fact proliferated over recent years. Indeed, conditioning paradigms have been successfully exploited to provide access to the cognitive products that such learning yields (Fenson, Zeedyk, & Vella, 1990; Vella & Zeedyk, 1990). For example, throughout the 1980s, Rovee-Collier and her colleagues made extensive use of the conjugate reinforcement technique for assessing long-term memory for operantly trained responses during the first year of life (Rovee-Collier, 1987; Rovee-Collier & Fagen, 1981; Rovee-Collier & Gekowski, 1979). However, with some exceptions (Fagen, 1977; McKirdy & Rovee, 1978; Rovee-Collier & Capatides, 1979), the conjugate reinforcement technique has been used primarily to study long-term retention processes rather than learning processes during behavior acquisition. That is, although this has been a successful and informative research program, its goal to this point has not included the study of the processes occurring within learning itself.

The Use of the Discrimination-Learning Task with Infants

In order to address these issues with infants, the discrimination-learning task has been recently employed with infants for the explicit purpose of exploring the processes involved in the acquisition of information (Colombo, Mitchell, Coldren, & Atwater, 1990). Clearly, methodological adaptations were required to make the task appropriate for use with infants. First, a response by which infants could indicate their choice of a particular stimulus had to be identified; second, a means of reinforcing that response had to be developed (Caron & Caron, 1978; Sameroff & Cavanaugh, 1979). Visual fixation—which has long been accepted as a reliable measure of processing in infancy—was chosen as the response measure. Given previously demonstrated constraints on infants' sensitivity to reinforcement (Millar, 1972; Watson, 1966, 1967), a reinforcer was needed that was immediate and that extended beyond a sudden discrete episode, lest infants fail to associate it with their response. Moreover, the choice of the reinforcer had to have some value to the infant and be appropriate to the child's age. An auditory event, such as natural speech, was chosen because this response-reinforcer pairing was felt to be one that infants would have experienced in their natural environment. Further, it was decided to present the auditory reinforcement synchronous with fixation (Colombo & Bundy, 1981, 1983; Ramey, Hieger, & Klisz, 1972; Watson, 1969).

In using this paradigm in an initial set of studies, 3-, 6-, and 9-month-old infants were presented with two distinct visual stimuli, and the presentations were made over series of 10-sec trials corresponding to four distinct phases. During a *baseline* phase containing four to eight trials, the pair of targets was presented and the duration of fixation on each target measured. During each trial of the subsequent *acquisition* phase, infants were reinforced for fixating on the target that had been less preferred during the baseline phase. Reinforcement was accomplished by presenting a brief recording of a female voice synchronous with the infant's fixation on this (previously nonpreferred) stimulus; that is, its onset coincided with the infant's fixation on the *correct* target and continued until the infant terminated the fixation.

Following acquisition, an *extinction* phase was administered in which reinforcement was withdrawn in order to observe whether the infants' fixation on the correct target continued in the absence of the reinforcer. Finally, during the *relearning* phase, reinforcement was reinstated for fixating on the same stimulus as during the initial learning phase.

Across all ages, the distribution of infants' visual fixations shifted to the reinforced target during the learning phase, decreased during the extinction phase, and rose again during the relearning phase. Following this initial set of studies, the synchronous reinforcement technique has been successfully used by other investigators to study such other cognitive processes involved in infants' learning as individual differences in fixation duration (Mitchell, 1990) and infants' detection of relations among objects that are either the same or different (Tyrrell, Minard, & Wass, 1992; Tyrrell, Zingaro, & Minard, 1992).

PREVIEW OF THE EXPERIMENTS

The development of a technology for conducting discrimination-learning research in preverbal infants provided the opportunity to test some of the basic theoretical issues concerning the contribution of mediation and attention processes to learning. Furthermore, it opened up the capacity for studying previously unexplored areas concerned with the operation of infants' attention processes during simple problem-solving tasks. The series of experiments reported in this *Monograph* was designed to extend the earlier basic findings on infants' performance during discrimination learning and to explore the contribution of specific cognitive mechanisms to success on such tasks.

The basic aim of the first two experiments (Chap. III) is to test fundamental predictions concerning the necessity of verbal processes for successful performance by examining preverbal infants' learning and transfer under conditions in which reinforcement is shifted from stimulus dimensions and features that were reinforced in initial training to alternate dimensions and features. The aim of the third and fourth experiments (Chap. IV) is to determine more precisely the nature of infants' representation and the processes guiding attention selection in these tasks. This is achieved (1) by testing whether infants attend to dimensions during initial training and whether this learning transfers to another problem containing new features on the same dimensions and (2) by examining whether infants' learning is discontinuous and whether the choice of a particular (dominant) stimulus dimension facilitates solution of the learning problem. We focused on 9-

month-olds in these experiments because they represent a population that is preverbal but that nevertheless possesses sophisticated attention abilities as indicated by their capacity to select and cognitively represent a variety of stimulus properties in static-task tests (Colombo, McCollam, et al., 1990; Colombo, Mitchell, et al., 1990; Husaim & Cohen, 1981; Younger, 1990; Younger & Cohen, 1986).

III. INFANTS' MEDIATION PROCESSES DURING LEARNING

This first set of experiments had two purposes. The first was to determine whether infants could learn to respond differentially to a particular stimulus feature under conditions where other stimulus features were also present and varying. Previous research had demonstrated infants' ability to learn to respond to a reinforced stimulus and to ignore irrelevant, nonreinforced stimuli. However, because these previous demonstrations typically presented and varied only two stimulus features in a single dimension (e.g., two colors or two forms), they provide little indication of infants' abilities to discriminate several covarying and competing stimulus dimensions and features. To generate such data, we simultaneously varied the stimuli presented to infants along the dimensions of color, form, texture, height, and position.

The second purpose was to address predictions of the mediation/level-of-functioning model of learning with preverbal subjects. As noted in Chapter II, the Kendler's mediation model predicted—as had been proposed by Spence—that subjects younger than 5 years old would learn by accumulating excitatory strength to the reinforced stimulus feature; performance through mediated or higher-level functioning could not occur without the presence of verbal ability or sufficient neurological maturation (Flavell, Beach, & Chinsky, 1966; Kendler, 1963; Reese, 1962).

The age-related changes in learning reported by the Kendlers (see the discussion in Chap. II) supported this position; however, it has never been directly tested with preverbal infants. Although previous work on infants has examined reversal shifts during learning (Papousek, 1967; Siqueland & Lipsitt, 1966; Weisberg & Simmons, 1966), such reversals were not designed to bear on the theoretical question of whether mediation is involved.

Our experiment directly examined the nature of learning during infancy, and the necessity of specific processes that it may involve, by testing infants' ability to perform reversal and nonreversal shifts. If, by virtue of their verbal immaturity, infants were to find R shifts more difficult than NR shifts, then Spence's (1936) and Kendler and Kendler's (1962) accounts of early learning in life would be supported. Alternatively, if infants proved able to solve R shifts more easily than NR shifts, then at least two different conclusions are possible.

First, mediation (be it verbal or any other kind) might in fact be irrelevant to mature performance on discrimination-learning tasks. Alternately, while some form of mediation might be involved in discrimination-learning performance, it is not verbal in nature. In either case, such results would indicate that verbal mediation is not involved in the dimension processing reflected in superiority of performance under R over NR shift conditions.

Undertaking such a test with infants also redresses Spence's (1956) complaint that his position was largely rejected on the basis of data obtained on verbally proficient college students when he had expressly designed the model to account for the behavior of nonverbal subjects.

EXPERIMENT 1:
REVERSAL AND NONREVERSAL SHIFT PERFORMANCE
IN 9-MONTH-OLD INFANTS

Method

Subjects

Names of parents and infants were obtained from public birth records for Johnson County, Kansas, a suburban area of Kansas City. Introductory letters were sent to parents explaining the study, followed by a phone call to schedule an appointment. Parents were not paid for participation. Forty-eight 9-month-old infants (24 males and 24 females) constituted the final sample; 10 additional infants were tested but excluded from the sample owing to fussiness ($N = 8$), sleepiness ($N = 1$), or interference from siblings ($N = 1$). The sample was predominantly Caucasian, healthy, and without known developmental abnormalities. More detailed characteristics of the sample are reported in Table 1.

TABLE 1

SAMPLE CHARACTERISTICS FOR EXPERIMENT 1

	M	SD	Min.	Max.
Infants:				
Testing age (weeks)	39.4	.9	36.0	41.7
Gestational age (weeks)	39.8	1.2	37.0	43.0
Birth weight (grams)	3,509.5	392.1	2,721.6	4,309.2
Mothers:				
Age (years)	31.1	3.8	23.0	39.0
Highest level of education (years) ..	15.3	2.1	12.0	20.0

Apparatus and Stimuli

Infants were brought to the laboratory by a parent and tested in a darkened 2 × 3-m cubicle that consisted of a black plywood front wall with a 1.0 × 0.7-m translucent Plexiglas screen mounted in the center. A video camera was concealed above the projection screen and a pair of loudspeakers positioned at the base of the front wall. The remaining three sides of the booth consisted of heavy black cloth.

To construct the stimuli, colored forms approximately 7.5 cm in height and width were cut from commercially available construction paper and centered on a 21.5 cm wide × 28 cm tall white background; these were then photographically reproduced and mounted in slides. Stimuli could vary along the dimensions of color (green vs. blue), form (triangle vs. circle), texture (hatched vs. plain), height (tall vs. short), and position (left vs. right). These particular dimensions were chosen because they have been widely employed in discrimination-learning research and because it is known that 9-month-olds have the sensory capacity to perceptually discriminate within each of these dimensions (Banks & Salapatek, 1983; Bornstein, 1984).

Infants were held on their parent's lap at a distance of approximately 1.5 m from the front screen. The parents were instructed to keep the infant seated if possible; if not, the infant was allowed to stand on the parent's lap. Parents were also asked not to talk to the infant or to point to the screen or any of the targets. Stimuli were rear-projected in pairs onto the translucent screen so that one appeared to the left and the other to the right of the infant's midline. Each stimulus slide in the pair subtended a visual angle of 24° (vertical) × 16° (horizontal) and was separated by 35° from the other stimulus.

An observer monitored infants' visual fixations through a 1.5-cm peephole located to the side of the screen. Whenever the observer saw the reflection of the stimulus on the infant's cornea, he or she depressed a hand-held button corresponding to that side. A Zenith Z-158 microcomputer was programmed in BASIC to record the fixations on-line and to control the presentation of the stimulus pairs. All observers were trained until they met or exceeded 95% agreement on fixation duration; such reliability has been found to be maintained over random assessments (see Colombo, Mitchell, et al., 1990).

Design and Procedure

Following Kendler and Kendler's (1959) mandatory-shift design, infants were randomly assigned to one of three shift conditions: *reversal* (R), *nonreversal* (NR), and *control* (C). Infants in the R and NR conditions were presented stimulus pairs that varied in color and form. As illustrated in

TABLE 2

	Correct Feature	Correct Dimension
Reversal shift		
Training phase:	Blue	Color
Trial 1 (green triangle, *blue circle*)		
Trial 2 (green circle, *blue triangle*)		
Test phase:	Green	Color
Trial 1 (*green triangle*, blue triangle)		
Trial 2 (*green circle*, blue circle)		
Nonreversal shift		
Training phase:	Blue	Color
Trial 1 (green triangle, *blue circle*)		
Trial 2 (green circle, *blue triangle*)		
Test phase:	Triangle	Form
Trial 1 (*green triangle*, green circle)		
Trial 2 (*blue triangle*, blue circle)		
Control shift		
Training phase:	Hatched	Texture
Trial 1 (*short hatched*, tall plain)		
Trial 2 (short plain, *tall hatched*)		
Test phase:	Green	Color
Trial 1 (*green triangle*, blue triangle)		
Trial 2 (*green circle*, blue circle)		

NOTE.—The reinforced stimulus is italicized.

Table 2, one stimulus pair contained a green triangle and a blue circle and another pair a green circle and a blue triangle. For infants in the C condition, the features of texture and height were also presented. One pair contained a tall hatched pink rectangle and short plain pink rectangle and the other a short hatched pink rectangle and tall plain pink rectangle.

In all, 16 trials, divided equally between training and test phases, were presented to each infant. During the *training phase,* infants in all three conditions were reinforced for visually fixating on a particular feature of the stimulus (the correct feature was designated a priori by the experimenter). Infants assigned to the R and NR conditions were initially trained to fixate on a particular feature of either color (green or blue) or form (triangle or circle); infants assigned to the control condition were initially trained to fixate on one of the features of texture (hatched or plain). The assignment of stimulus features to which fixation was reinforced was balanced equally across subjects. Further, stimulus pairs were presented so that no stimulus feature appeared in the same consecutive position for more than two trials, and the sides on which the features appeared were also balanced within subjects. Observers were unaware of the experimental condition to which the infant was assigned, and their placement behind and to the side of the projection screen precluded them seeing the display shown to the infant during the testing session.

Every time the infant fixated on the designated stimulus in the pair, auditory reinforcement (a recording of a woman talking) was presented synchronously with the onset and duration of the infant's fixation (following Colombo, Mitchell, et al., 1990). When the observer depressed the button indicating that the infant was looking toward the target designated as correct, the computer closed a relay to allow the auditory track to be heard through the speakers. Each trial lasted until the infant accumulated 10 sec of looking time toward one or both of the targets in the pair, at which time the trial was terminated and the stimulus screen went blank. A delay of approximately 1 sec occurred while slides were advanced automatically for the next trial in the training phase.

Following a delay of 4 sec while the slide trays were reset by an experimenter, eight trials constituting the *test phase* were then initiated. In this phase, the reinforcement contingencies were *shifted* (see Table 2). For infants assigned to the R condition, fixation on the other feature in the same dimension was now reinforced (e.g., if an infant had been trained to fixate on blue, green was reinforced after the shift). For the NR condition, fixation on a feature on the other dimension was reinforced (e.g., if an infant had been trained to fixate on blue, postshift looking toward the form of either the triangle or the circle was reinforced). The assignment of stimulus features to be reinforced during the test phase was balanced across subjects, and all possible combinations of features were reinforced across the training and test phases.

For the test phase in the C condition (in which training was on the dimension of texture), infants were presented with the same stimulus pairs as those shown to the R and NR groups, and looking toward a feature of color (green or blue) or of form (triangle or circle) was reinforced. The rationale behind the inclusion of the control group was to provide a comparison in which there should be theoretically no transfer effects from the training phase, thus allowing assessment of the relative difficulty of the R and NR conditions. Thus, this group experienced a contingency shift that was neither R nor NR with respect to the training phase.

An important difference between the training and test phases was the number of dimensions that varied per trial (see Table 2). In the training phase, two dimensions varied per trial (color and form). However, in the test phase, the irrelevant dimension was held constant on any single trial. This type of presentation of the irrelevant dimension has been referred to as *variable between trials* or *constant within trials* (Dickerson, Wagner, & Campione, 1970; Esposito, 1975). The logic for this restriction was to avoid inadvertent reinforcement of a previously correct response from the training phase: if the irrelevant dimension varies during the shift phase, it has been argued that effects due to partial reinforcement may actually impede the learning of NRs (Buss, 1953, 1956; Kelleher, 1956; Kendler & Kendler, 1959). For example, if the color blue was reinforced during the training phase, then, during an NR shift to a form feature, a blue form reinforced in half the test trials might cause the subject to persist in choosing a blue feature instead of learning a response based on having reinforcement shifted to the form feature. Thus, if infants' performance on these two types of shifts are to be contrasted, effects due to partial reinforcement should be minimized (Eimas, 1965; Esposito, 1975; Slamecka, 1968).

Results

Data Reduction

The proportions of time that infants fixated on the reinforced feature during 10-sec trials were averaged across four adjacent trials into *blocks,* each of which represents the presentation of the reinforced feature across every possible irrelevant feature (see Fig. 2).

Preliminary Analyses

A between-subjects MANOVA run to determine whether there were any differences across the four trial blocks due to the infants' sex yielded nonsignificant results ($F[4, 41] = 2.44$, $p = $ N.S.); hence, the infants' sex was not included in further analyses.

Overall Analysis

A 3 (condition: R/NR/C) × 2 (phase: train/test) × 2 (block) mixed-model ANOVA yielded a significant three-way interaction ($F[2, 43] = 9.51$, $p < .001$) as well as a significant main effect for block ($F[1, 43] = 22.44$, $p < .001$). To decompose these effects, each phase of the procedure was analyzed separately.[1]

Training-Phase Analyses

A two-way mixed-model ANOVA was conducted on the training-phase data involving the factors of block (2) and condition (3: R/NR/C). A signifi-

---

[1] This strategy for analysis was determined a priori and was based directly on our hypotheses. According to Keppel (1991), this approach is not inadvisable.

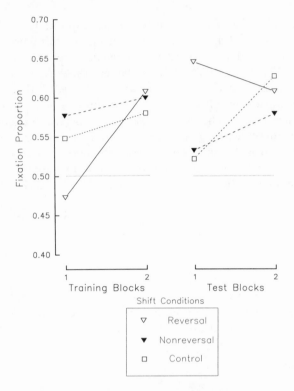

Fig. 2.—Experiment 1: Proportion of time per trial block that infants spent fixating on the relevant stimulus feature during training and reversal (R) or nonreversal (NR) shifts. The chance level (μ) is represented by the dotted line at .50.

cant main effect was found for block ($F[1, 45] = 23.34, p < .001$), indicating that the proportion of time that infants spent fixating increased as they acquired the contingency. However, this main effect was qualified by a significant two-way interaction between the factors ($F[2, 45] = 7.74, p < .01$), which was attributable to the fact that infants in the R condition fixated on the reinforced target less during the trials composing the first trial block than infants in the other two conditions. As a result of the lowered initial level of fixation in the R condition, only these infants showed a significant increase in fixation across blocks ($t[15] = 6.61, p < .001$).

In addition, each of the trial block data points was also tested against the theoretical chance level (μ) of .50. Infants' fixation in the R condition differed from chance in the second training block ($t[15] = 6.21, p < .001$). For infants in the NR condition, fixation was significantly different from μ on both the first ($t[15] = 2.80, p < .05$) and the second ($t[15] = 5.43, p < .001$) blocks, whereas infants in the C condition did not differ from chance on either training block.

Preferences for stimulus features.—Several previous studies have explored children's preferences for certain stimulus features in discrimination-learning tasks and, specifically, in R and NR shift paradigms (Caron, 1969; Kendler & Kendler, 1959; Offenbach, 1979; Smiley & Weir, 1966). To determine whether infants in our sample preferentially fixated on certain color or form features over others during training, two ANOVAs were conducted. Separate ANOVAs were necessary because, by design, the features were not completely counterbalanced across the three shift conditions: the features of green, blue, triangle, and circle were presented to infants in the R and NR condition, whereas infants in the C condition were presented with the features of stripes, plain, short, and tall (during the training phase).

The first analysis consisted of a three-way mixed-model ANOVA including the factors block (2), shift condition (2: R/NR), and training feature (4: blue/green/triangle/circle). As in the previous analysis, significant main effects were observed for the shift condition ($F[1, 24] = 5.90, p < .05$) and for the blocks ($F[1, 24] = 33.57, p < .001$) factors, which were qualified by a significant condition $\times$ blocks interaction ($F[1, 24] = 17.46, p < .001$). Moreover, a significant main effect of stimulus feature was also found ($F[3, 24] = 10.26, p < .001$). A follow-up one-way ANOVA ($F[3, 28] = 9.21, p < .001$) with Scheffé multiple range tests revealed that circle ($M = .65$) was fixated on significantly more ($p < .05$) than blue ($M = .54$), green ($M = .52$), or triangle ($M = .53$). It is important to recognize that the feature factor did not enter into any significant interactions with the blocks or the shift condition factors: even though the circle was fixated on for the greatest proportion of time, infants in both the shift conditions increased their fixation on all features during the second block of training trials.

The second analysis conducted on infants in the C condition involved a two-way mixed-model 2 (training feature: stripes vs. plain) $\times$ 2 (blocks) ANOVA. The only significant result was a main effect of feature ($F[1, 14] = 95.54, p < .001$), with stripes ($M = .71$) being fixated on for significantly greater proportions of time than plain ($M = .40$). This disparity in fixation on the individual features of the control stimuli undoubtedly contributed to the variance in responding that explains the lower level of fixation observed for infants in this condition during the training phase.

Test-Phase Analyses

A block (2) $\times$ condition (3: R/NR/C) mixed-model ANOVA performed on fixation time during the test phase revealed significant main effects for both factors (block, $F[1, 43] = 4.10, p < .05$; condition, $F[2, 43] = 4.02, p < .05$) as well as a significant interaction between the two ($F[2, 43] = 4.88, p < .05$). The source of the interaction was analyzed by testing for effects due to shift condition in a one-way ANOVA for each test block. A significant effect of the shift condition was found only for the first test block ($F[2, 45] = 9.10, p < .001$). Follow-up Scheffé range tests indicated that fixation time in the R shift condition was significantly higher than in the NR or C conditions ($p < .05$). Thus, infants in the R condition had little difficulty shifting their fixation on the new reinforced feature at the outset of the shift phase, whereas infants in the NR and C groups fixated on the new reinforced feature at a lower level.

The results of the ANOVA were complemented by t tests of the durations of fixation against chance (.50). During the first test block, only infants in the R condition fixated on the reinforced stimulus feature at a level above chance ($t[15] = 4.77, p < .001$). In the second test block, infants in all three conditions showed fixation time significantly above chance (R, $t[14] = 4.25$, $p < .001$; NR, $t[15] = 2.63, p < .05$; C, $t[14] = 6.84, p < .001$). Thus, both this analysis and the ANOVA presented above indicate that infants performed R shifts with greater ease than either NR or C shifts.

Preferences for stimulus features.—To determine whether infants preferentially fixated on certain colors or forms during the test phase, a three-way mixed-model ANOVA was conducted across the block (2), shift condition (3: R/NR/C), and feature (4: blue/green/triangle/circle) factors. Significant main effects were obtained for the shift condition ($F[2, 34] = 4.32, p < .05$) and the condition × blocks interaction ($F[2, 34] = 5.45, p < .01$); however, the stimulus feature factor was nonsignificant ($F[3, 34] = 2.82, p = $ N.S.).

Discussion

This experiment yielded two findings that have not been investigated to date with this age range. First, infants learned to fixate on a particular stimulus feature that was associated with reinforcement in the presence of two other features that were present and varying. Thus, by 9 months of age, infants can discriminate individual stimulus features in compounds that vary in color, form, and position; as they learned which of the features was associated with reinforcement, their differential fixation on this feature increased across trials.

The second noteworthy finding is that infants in the R group had the highest duration of fixation on the new reinforced stimulus feature immediately following the shift procedure; infants in the NR and C groups fixated on the new reinforced stimulus at a lower level. The higher level of fixation during the R shift suggests that infants learned to respond to the relevant *dimension* (e.g., color) rather than just to an isolated component (e.g., blue); recall that, in an R shift, the same dimension is relevant in both the training and the test phases and that only the response to the specific reinforced feature needs to be altered. Likewise, the lower level of fixation observed for infants in the NR shift condition suggests that they too learned to fixate on the reinforced dimension during the learning phase of the procedure; such learning interfered with their performance during the shift phase.

This pattern of findings contrasts with what both Spence and the Kendlers would predict. As noted previously, the prediction from Kendler and Kendler's (1962) developmental model of discrimination learning maintained that subjects younger than 5 years of age (which clearly includes infants) would encode stimulus components nonselectively through a continuous, associational learning process. Justification for this prediction was expected to be seen in a higher proportion of fixation following the NR shift than the R shift. Instead, however, our results revealed just the opposite. The superior performance of the R group, which indicates learning of dimensions rather than of specific features, suggests some form of mediation, a process that the Kendlers assumed to be possible only after the acquisition of language. Since 9-month-olds lack the ability for verbal representation, some other form of mediation must be operative. The experiment that we report next was designed as an attempt to replicate the finding before moving to attempts to determine the nature of such a mediation process.

EXPERIMENT 2:
REVERSAL AND NONREVERSAL SHIFT PERFORMANCE
IN 9-MONTH-OLD INFANTS WITH THE IRRELEVANT DIMENSION
VARIABLE WITHIN TRIALS

The results of Experiment 1 unexpectedly indicated that infants perform R shifts with greater ease than NR shifts, thus suggesting that they are able to respond to abstract dimensions of the stimuli (e.g., color and form) in the absence of language skills. However, in order to accept this conclusion safely, it is necessary to rule out any factors that might provide alternative explanations of this surprising finding.

One confound that has caused significant difficulties in interpreting subjects' performance in the R/NR shift task in the past involves whether the irrelevant dimension is varied or kept constant within the trials of the shift (test) phase (Shepp & Turrisi, 1966; Slamecka, 1968; Wolff, 1967). In Experiment 1, we varied only the relevant dimension, following Kendler and Kendler's (1959) reasoning that, unless the irrelevant dimension was kept constant, effects due to partial reinforcement may render infants' learning in the NR condition more difficult (e.g., Buss, 1953, 1956).

However, questions have been raised about whether this type of stimulus presentation yields the most unambiguous interpretation of results from the various shift conditions (Esposito, 1975; Slamecka, 1968). Contrary to the Kendlers, it has been argued that keeping the irrelevant dimension constant within trials may make the NR rather than the R shift easier (e.g., Eimas, 1965). The reasoning here is that, in the initial learning phase of a discrimination-learning task containing, for example, color and form dimensions, the subject presumably learns to respond to the relevant dimension—say, color—in solving this phase of the problem. If, in the subsequent NR shift, color—which is now the irrelevant dimension—is held constant within trials, the problem may be easier to solve because the subject is essentially forced to respond to the features of the new relevant dimension. Of course, the subject still faces the difficulty of having to respond to one of the relevant individual features within the new relevant dimension. Experiments designed to investigate subjects' performance under various shift conditions by manipulating the presentation of the irrelevant dimension to be either constant or variable within trials have yielded equivocal results (Caron, 1969, 1970; Dickerson et al., 1970; Tighe & Tighe, 1965, 1967).

Because of these uncertainties, the purpose of Experiment 2 was to investigate the effect of having both the relevant and the irrelevant dimensions vary within the test-phase trials on the performance of 9-month-olds in R and NR shifts. The results have a direct bearing on whether the findings of Experiment 1 can be properly attributed to subjects' abstraction of dimensions or whether they are due to having kept the irrelevant constant in the test phase.

Method

Subjects

Subjects were recruited in the same manner as for Experiment 1. Forty-eight 9-month-old infants (24 males and 24 females) composed the final sample; 17 additional infants were tested but excluded owing to fussiness ($N = 13$), interference from the mother during testing ($N = 3$), or prematurity ($N = 1$). The sample was predominantly Caucasian, healthy, and without known developmental abnormalities. More detailed characteristics of the sample are reported in Table 3.

Apparatus and Stimuli

The apparatus and stimuli were identical to those used in Experiment 1.

TABLE 3

SAMPLE CHARACTERISTICS FOR EXPERIMENT 2

	M	SD	Min.	Max.
Infants:				
Testing age (weeks)	39.6	.8	38.6	41.9
Gestational age (weeks)	39.8	1.2	37.0	42.0
Birth weight (grams)	3,687.6	622.5	2,579.8	6,548.8
Mothers:				
Age (years)	30.4	3.5	21.0	37.0
Highest level of education (years) ..	15.2	1.7	12.0	18.0

Design and Procedure

The design was identical to that of Experiment 1, with the sole exception that both the relevant and the irrelevant dimensions varied within trials during the test phase of each shift condition (see Table 4).

Results

Data Reduction and Preliminary Analyses

Once again, data on the proportion of time that infants fixated on the reinforced feature during each 10-sec trial were averaged across four adjacent trials into blocks (see Fig. 3). As in Experiment 1, a between-subjects MANOVA run to determine whether there were any differences across the four trial blocks due to sex of the infants proved nonsignificant ($F[4, 43]$ = .512, p = N.S.); sex was therefore not included in further analyses.

Overall Analysis

A 3 (condition: R/NR/C) × 2 (phase: training/test) × 2 (block) mixed-model ANOVA yielded only a marginally significant main effect for block ($F[1, 45]$ = 2.86, $p < .10$). Because further probing of the data is thus unwarranted, the only additional analyses sought to determine whether the data points differ from chance levels by testing them against μ (.50).

Tests against Chance

Training phase.—For infants in the R condition, fixation was significantly above chance in both training blocks (block 1, $t[15]$ = 3.27, $p < .01$; block 2, $t[15]$ = 2.79, $p < .05$). For infants in the NR condition, it was

TABLE 4

Shifts and Stimulus Presentations Used in Experiment 2,
as Illustrated by the First Two Trials

	Correct Feature	Correct Dimension
Reversal shift		
Training phase:	Blue	Color
Trial 1 (green triangle, *blue circle*)		
Trial 2 (green circle, *blue triangle*)		
Test phase:	Green	Color
Trial 1 (*green triangle*, blue circle)		
Trial 2 (*green circle*, blue triangle)		
Nonreversal shift		
Training phase:	Blue	Color
Trial 1 (green triangle, *blue circle*)		
Trial 2 (green circle, *blue triangle*)		
Test phase:	Triangle	Form
Trial 1 (*green triangle*, blue circle)		
Trial 2 (green circle, *blue triangle*)		
Control shift		
Training phase:	Hatched	Texture
Trial 1 (*short hatched*, tall plain)		
Trial 2 (short plain, *tall hatched*)		
Test phase:	Green	Color
Trial 1 (*green triangle*, blue circle)		
Trial 2 (*green circle*, blue triangle)		

Note.—The reinforced stimulus is italicized.

significantly different from μ on only the second ($t[15] = 2.88$, $p < .05$) block, and, for those in the C condition, it did not differ from chance on either block.

Test phase.—During the first test block, infants in the R and C conditions fixated on the reinforced stimulus feature at a level above chance ($t[15] = 4.67$, $p < .001$; $t[15] = 2.82$, $p < .05$, respectively). During the second block, duration of fixation was significantly above chance for infants in the NR ($t[15] = 3.36$, $p < .01$) and C ($t[15] = 2.17$, $p < .05$) conditions.

Discussion

As in Experiment 1, the results of this experiment indicated that infants learned to discriminate a particular stimulus feature associated with auditory reinforcement from the nexus of features presented in the various compounds. However, the statistics did not precisely replicate the earlier findings concerning infants' performance in the shift phase of the proce-

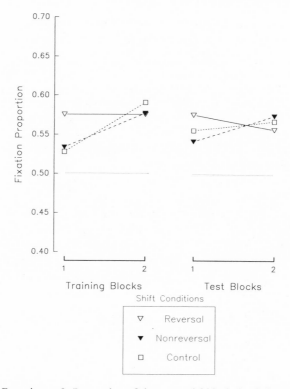

Fig. 3.—Experiment 2: Proportion of time per trial block that infants spent fixating on the relevant stimulus feature during training and reversal (R) or nonreversal (NR) shifts under conditions in which two irrelevant dimensions varied *within* trials during the test phase. The chance level (μ) is represented by the dotted line at .50.

dure. As in Experiment 1, infants in the R condition showed longer durations of fixation during the first block of the test trials than those in the NR group (see Fig. 3), again suggesting that their performance was facilitated by being able to discriminate and attend to a dimension of the stimuli and to transfer attention to that dimension in the shift phase. Although evident in the graphic display, this pattern did not emerge as statistically significant in the ANOVA. However, tests of the individual data points against μ (.50) clearly indicated that the performance of infants in the R condition immediately after the shift in reinforcement was statistically above chance levels while that of infants in the NR shift condition was not.

Comparison of the data plotted in Figures 2 and 3 suggests that, when the number of dimensions permitted to vary within trials is increased during the test phase (two in Experiment 2 vs. one in Experiment 1), all shifts are performed at lower levels of fixation. This finding is not surprising since well-documented reports that attention to a particular dimension decreases as the number of irrelevant dimensions increases are available in the literature (Trabasso & Bower, 1968). From this reasoning, the duration of fixation in Experiment 1 was higher because, with fewer dimensions varying during the shift trials, it was relatively easier for infants to isolate the relevant dimension. However, as the number of irrelevant dimensions increases, it is more difficult for infants to transfer and attend to the relevant dimension when another dimension is present and varying. Thus, in terms of the question whether the number of dimensions that vary during the test phase affects the ease with which R or NR shifts are performed (Eimas, 1965), the results of this experiment indicate that all groups are adversely affected when the number of varying dimensions is increased. Note, however, that examining the results across Experiments 1 and 2 indicates that no particular shift condition seems to benefit or suffer by changing the number of varying dimensions.

The question that this experiment set out to resolve was whether the pattern of findings that we obtained in Experiment 1, and interpreted as suggesting that some process of internal mediation underlies infants' discrimination learning, could be an artifact of the stimulus presentation. The results of the current experiment clearly indicate that explanations in terms of the latter are unlikely.

IV. THE NATURE AND PROCESSES INVOLVED
IN INFANTS' LEARNING

The results thus far indicate that infants discriminate particular reinforced features within a relatively complex stimulus array. Moreover, the longer durations of fixation obtained under R shift conditions in both experiments indicate that infants process compound stimuli in terms of their dimensions, that is, that they transfer their learning freely from one feature to another within a reinforced dimension, even though the specific feature to which reinforcement was shifted had never been directly reinforced previously.

This attention to a dimension facilitates learning where, as in an R shift, the same dimension remains relevant. Unfortunately, because the R and NR shift tasks involve presentation of the same stimulus features and dimensions during both the training and the shift phases, the effects of attention to a dimension cannot be precisely distinguished from the effects of partial reinforcement of a particular stimulus feature. What is clear, however, is that, since the infant subjects of the present study were preverbal, verbal mediation must be dismissed as being a necessary condition for abstraction of the relevant dimension information.

EXPERIMENT 3:
INTRADIMENSION/EXTRADIMENSION SHIFT PERFORMANCE
IN 9-MONTH-OLD INFANTS

The purpose of our third experiment was to test directly the hypothesis that infants discriminate and attend to *dimensions* during learning. As noted earlier, in advancing their attention model, Zeaman and House (1963) proposed that a crucial step in solving a discrimination-learning problem involves an initial orienting response (OR) to the relevant dimension of the stimuli. This proposition has been extensively tested with the intradimension/extradimension (ID/ED) shift task (see Fig. 1 above); the paradigm is referred to as the *total change design*. The critical feature of this design is that, after training on a stimulus feature, the stimulus dimension is represented by a different feature during the shift phase. This manipulation allows attribution of any positive transfer across the two phases to a response based on stimulus dimensions rather than on isolated stimulus features that were learned during the training phase; thus, the methodological problems related to the presentation of the dimensions in the shift phase of the task that plague interpretation of the original R/NR paradigm are practically eliminated (see Eimas, 1965; Shepp & Turrisi, 1966; Slamecka, 1968). Hence, if infants were found to execute ID shifts with greater ease than they do ED shifts, we could conclude unambiguously that transfer of responding should be ascribed to attention to a dimension during information acquisition.

Such a finding would also be significant in extending the developmental implications of Zeaman and House's model to very young ages. The attention model posits that the orienting response does not change fundamentally as development proceeds (Dickerson et al., 1972; Eimas, 1967; Zeaman & House, 1974; cf. Kendler & Kendler, 1962), an assertion supported by showing that subjects over a wide range of ages perform an ID shift in fewer trials than an ED shift (Reese & Lipsitt, 1970; Shepp & Turrisi, 1966; Slamecka, 1968; Wolff, 1967). However, the attention model did not specify how the OR operated at ages younger than approximately 3–4 years (Zeaman & House, 1974).

There are several theoretical reasons to assume that an OR does operate during infancy. The best known is Sokolov's (1963) account of habituation of the visual OR in terms of a neuronal model (Cohen, DeLoache, & Strauss, 1979; Horowitz, 1974), in which he suggested that, once a stimulus or an environmental event occurs, the organism will respond by orienting to the stimulus—the organism stores a neuronal trace of the stimulus in the central nervous system. Sokolov's conceptualization is theoretically compatible with that of Zeaman and House: both models specify that part of the OR is a central component in the cognitive functioning of infants (Horowitz, 1969). Further theoretical convergence between these two models comes from Fagan's (1977) adaptation of Zeaman and House's model to describe infants' performance in the paired-comparison procedure. Concisely stated, Fagan posited that an essential part of infants' ability to discriminate a novel from a familiar stimulus is their ability to make an OR to the dimension containing the novel feature.

In terms of developmental research, there is already some evidence that infants are able to perceive a common element among a series of stimuli. Colombo, McCollam, et al. (1990) habituated 10-month-old infants to leaf forms; when the leaf color was varied during habituation to the leaf forms, introduction of a new color during the test phase was not regarded by the subjects as a novel event, leading the authors to conclude that infants

TABLE 5

SAMPLE CHARACTERISTICS FOR EXPERIMENT 3

	M	SD	Min.	Max.
Infants:				
Testing age (weeks)	39.6	1.0	38.6	43.6
Gestational age (weeks)	40.0	1.3	36.0	42.0
Birth weight (grams)	3,658.1	473.5	2,664.9	4,989.6
Mothers:				
Age (years)	31.4	3.8	21.0	38.0
Highest level of education (years) ..	15.2	1.9	12.0	18.0

responded to color as a dimension that is indexed by any one of a set of features.

Taken together, these studies give substantial reason to believe that even very young infants selectively attend to the dimensions of color and form. The present experiment was designed to provide the first direct test of this assertion by directly reinforcing infants' attention to a stimulus feature within a particular dimension and then examining whether their performance is facilitated in another problem in which that same dimension is relevant.

Method

Subjects

Subjects were recruited in the same manner as in the two previous experiments. Sixty-four 9-month-olds (27 males and 37 females) composed the final sample; 10 additional infants were tested but excluded owing to fussiness ($N = 4$), equipment malfunction ($N = 2$), experimenter error ($N = 2$), prematurity ($N = 1$), or apparent strabismus ($N = 1$). The sample was predominantly Caucasian, healthy, and without known developmental abnormalities. More detailed characteristics of the sample are reported in Table 5.

Apparatus and Stimuli

The apparatus was identical to that used in Experiments 1 and 2. However, the design required that a set of stimuli containing new features for the dimensions of color and form be constructed. On the color dimension, the new features were red and orange; the new features on the form dimension were a square and a plus sign.

Design and Procedure

As in the previous two experiments, infants were presented with stimulus pairs that varied in terms of color and form features, and the reinforcement contingencies were systematically shifted across the training and test phases; however, the nature of the shifts differed in some important ways. Infants were assigned to either an ID or an ED shift condition. As shown in Table 6, one training stimulus pair contained a green triangle and a blue circle and the other a green circle and a blue triangle.

A total of eight training trials and eight test trials were presented. During the training phase, infants in both conditions were reinforced for visually fixating on a particular stimulus feature; the assignment of individual stimulus features to be trained was balanced equally across subjects. Further, stimulus pairs were presented so that no stimulus feature appeared in the same position for more than two consecutive trials; the side on which the feature initially appeared was also balanced across subjects. Half the subjects were initially trained to blue/green and circle/triangle and the other half to red/orange and square/plus. Every time the infant fixated on the designated stimulus in the pair, auditory reinforcement of a woman talking was again presented synchronously with the onset and duration of the infants' fixation on the stimulus. Each trial lasted until the infant accumulated 10 sec of looking time to one or to both of the targets in the pair.

In the subsequent eight test-phase trials, the reinforcement contingen-

TABLE 6

SHIFTS AND STIMULUS PRESENTATIONS USED IN EXPERIMENT 3,
AS ILLUSTRATED BY THE FIRST TWO TRIALS

	Correct Feature	Correct Dimension
Intradimensional (ID) shift		
Training phase:	Blue	Color
Trial 1 (green triangle, *blue circle*)		
Trial 2 (green circle, *blue triangle*)		
Test phase:	Red	Color
Trial 1 (*red plus*, orange square)		
Trial 2 (*red square*, orange plus)		
Extradimensional (ED) shift		
Training phase:	Blue	Color
Trial 1 (green triangle, *blue circle*)		
Trial 2 (green circle, *blue triangle*)		
Test phase:	Plus	Form
Trial 1 (*red plus*, orange square)		
Trial 2 (red square, *orange plus*)		

NOTE.—The reinforced stimulus is italicized.

cies were shifted as shown in Table 6. The stimuli employed during this shift phase still varied along the dimensions of color and form, but the features of each of those were novel with respect to the training phase. For example, when the colors blue and green were employed during the training phase, the colors red and orange were employed during the test phase. Similarly, when triangle and circle were the forms employed during the training phase, square and plus forms were employed during the test phase.

As shown in Table 6, one stimulus test pair contained a red square and a orange plus sign and the other a red plus sign and an orange square. For infants assigned to the ID shift condition, consistent reinforcement was given for visually fixating on a stimulus feature within the same dimension as had been relevant during the training phase; for those in the ED shift condition, reinforcement was given for fixating on a feature of the dimension that had been irrelevant during training. The assignment of stimulus features to be reinforced during the test phase was balanced across subjects; moreover, all possible combinations of features were reinforced across the training and test phases.

A separate control group was not necessary because completely novel features of the dimensions were used during the shift phases; hence, the ED condition served to provide a group that could not benefit from positive transfer from the training phase.

Results

Data Reduction

As in the previous experiments, the proportions of time that infants fixated on the reinforced feature per 10-sec trial were averaged across every four adjacent trials into blocks (see Fig. 4), and data analysis proceeded as in Experiment 1.

Preliminary Analyses

A between-subjects MANOVA was run to determine whether there were any differences across the four trial blocks due to infants' sex. The results were nonsignificant ($F[4, 58] = .926$, $p = $ N.S.); consequently, the infants' sex was not included as a factor in subsequent analyses.

Overall Analysis

A 2 (condition: ID/ED) × 2 (phase: train/test) × 2 (block) mixed-model ANOVA yielded a significant three-way interaction ($F[1, 61] = 8.23$, $p <$

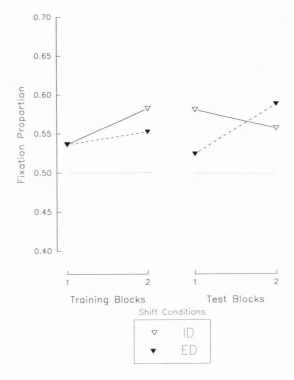

Fig. 4.—Experiment 3: Proportion of time per trial block that infants spent fixating on the relevant stimulus feature during training and intradimension (ID) or extradimension (ED) shifts. The chance level (μ) is represented by the dotted line at .50.

.01) as well as a significant main effect due to the blocks factor ($F[1, 61] = 4.72$, $p < .05$). As previously, the two phases of the procedure were then analyzed separately to decompose these effects.

Training-Phase Analyses

A two-way mixed-model ANOVA employing the factors of blocks (2) and condition (ID/ED) yielded a significant main effect for blocks ($F[1, 62] = 4.90$, $p < .05$); infants' proportion of fixation time increased from the first ($M = .54$) to the second ($M = .57$) training block as they learned the association between fixating on the stimulus and reinforcement. Infants in the ID condition fixated on the reinforced feature at levels above chance during the second training block ($t[31] = 4.20$, $p < .001$), whereas infants in the ED condition showed significant above-chance responding in the first block as well (block 1, $t[31] = 2.08$, $p < .05$; block 2, $t[31] = 2.64$, $p < .05$).

Preferences for stimulus features.—In order to determine whether infants preferentially fixated on certain colors or forms during training, a three-way mixed-model ANOVA including the factors block (2), condition (2: ID/ED), and training feature (8: blue/green/red/orange/triangle/circle/plus/square) was performed. As above, significant main effects were observed for the block factor ($F[1, 48] = 4.37, p < .05$); additionally, there was a significant main effect of stimulus feature ($F[7, 48] = 8.31, p < .001$). A follow-up one-way ANOVA ($F[7, 56] = 7.60, p < .001$) with Scheffé multiple range tests revealed that the plus sign ($M = .65$), the circle ($M = .60$), and the color blue ($M = .58$) were fixated on longer ($p < .05$) than the square ($M = .44$) and the triangle ($M = .48$). However, it should be noted that, since the stimulus feature factor did not enter into any significant interactions with either the block or the shift condition factors, these preferences had no bearing on infants' learning over blocks or on their performance during the shift condition.

Test-Phase Analyses

A 2 (blocks) × 2 (condition: ID/ED) mixed-model ANOVA revealed a significant two-way interaction ($F[1, 61] = 6.56, p < .05$), which was then decomposed via t tests of differences between the two shift conditions in each block. The difference proved significant for the first test block ($t[62] = 2.01, p < .05$); infants in the ID condition ($M = .58$) had longer fixations than those in the ED condition ($M = .52$).

This finding was bolstered by tests of fixation durations against chance; on the first test block, only infants in the ID condition showed durations of fixation that were significantly above chance ($t[31] = 4.34., p < .001$). On the second test block, however, infants in both conditions fixated on the reinforced target for durations significantly longer than chance (ID, $t[30] = 2.33, p < .05$; ED, $t[31] = 5.01, p < .001$).

Preferences for stimulus features.—A three-way mixed-model 2 (block) × 2 (condition: ID/ED) × 8 (test feature: blue/green/red/orange/triangle/circle/plus/square) ANOVA was conducted on the test-phase data. Replicating results obtained for the training phase, both the condition × block interaction ($F[1, 47] = 6.67, p < .05$) and stimulus test feature main effect ($F[7, 47] = 13.21, p < .001$) were significant. A follow-up one-way ANOVA ($F[7, 55] = 12.83, p < .001$) with Scheffé multiple range tests revealed that the plus sign ($M = .68$), the colors red ($M = .61$) and blue ($M = .60$), and the circle ($M = .60$) were fixated on significantly longer ($p < .05$) than the colors orange ($M = .56$) and green ($M = .53$), the square ($M = .47$), and the triangle ($M = .45$). Once again, the fact that this factor did not enter into any significant interactions with the blocks or the shift condition factors indicates that these preferences do not bear on conclusions drawn regarding the differences between the shift conditions.

Discussion

The results of our third experiment suggest that infants learned to respond to new features of a previously trained dimension with greater ease than to new features of a dimension that had not been previously trained. Theoretically, these results are significant because they are the first to demonstrate that preverbal infants selectively attend to compound stimuli in terms of abstract dimensions (such as color and form), in accordance with Zeaman and House's (1963) attention theory of discrimination learning. Moreover, the relative ease with which infants transferred responding to a dimension even when reinforcement was shifted to features that were completely novel replicates and extends the implication of the first two experiments, namely, that verbal mediation processes do not necessarily underlie the stimulus selection and processing that are seen in mature forms of discontinuous learning. It appears more reasonable to propose instead that a centrally based attention component is involved in infants' ability to solve visual discrimination-learning problems. This possibility is addressed in the fourth and final experiment in this program of research.

EXPERIMENT 4:
SELECTIVE ATTENTION AND SPEED OF
9-MONTH-OLD INFANTS' LEARNING PERFORMANCE

The results of the prior three experiments indicate that infants can learn to fixate on a particular reinforced stimulus feature within an array of other, varying stimulus features. Further, the results of the shifts in reinforcement conditions have consistently suggested that learning involves abstracting the dimensions of the stimulus from the reinforced features rather than a gradual accumulation of response strength to the individual features. Although many experiments have documented subjects' superior performance in ID over ED shifts across a wide range of ages and species (see Reese & Lipsitt, 1970), this superiority had never been established for subjects as young as those tested in our studies. Our findings thus extend the developmental implications of the attention model to suggest that the OR functions during infancy in ways similar to those in which it operates for older subjects (Zeaman & House, 1974).

An intriguing implication that this attention model holds for infants' discrimination learning is that the manner in which the subjects distribute their attention to the stimulus dimensions should predict their performance. Our findings that R and ID shifts were performed with ease clearly imply that infants do not learn nonselectively, as had been initially predicted by the Kendlers for subjects younger than 5 years of age. Instead, the present results correspond to the attention model, in which Zeaman and House (1963) proposed that the learning of discriminations proceeds in a discontinuous manner and that such learning is not possible until the subject has attentionally isolated those stimulus dimensions and features that consistently lead to reinforcement.

A corollary of this position is that subjects who are able to locate a relevant dimension quickly will also manifest more rapid learning than those who are unable to do so; for the latter, learning performance should hover around chance levels for a longer period. Regardless of the length of the presolution period, however, both types of subjects should show a precipitous rise in performance once the relevant dimension is finally isolated. The Zeaman and House model also explicitly predicted that the process of isolating the relevant stimulus feature occurred through sampling each stimulus dimension individually and sequentially. This position is compatible with the claim—initially advanced in the late 1920s—that subjects isolate the relevant dimension through an active selection process and that solutions to discrimination-learning tasks are consequently reached through selection and testing of various stimulus features (Bower & Trabasso, 1964; Krechevsky, 1932b).

The first aim of our final experiment was to test directly whether infants learn in the discontinuous manner that is characteristic of older children and adults. Such a test can be achieved by plotting backward learning curves so as to determine whether infants' probability of responding to the correct stimulus hovers around chance levels (i.e., 50% fixation time) and then rises dramatically just prior to attainment of the criterion (Hayes, 1953; Zeaman & House, 1963).

The only data to date to support the discontinuous nature of infant learning came from a recent set of experiments in which 3-, 6-, and 9-month-old infants were presented with pairs of visual stimuli containing a checkerboard and a bull's-eye (Colombo, Mitchell, et al., 1990). To determine whether infants' learning proceeded in a discontinuous or continuous fashion, the authors plotted the percentage fixation time directed toward the reinforced target over the learning phase trials *backward* from the point at which the subject's duration of fixation was 50% above initial baseline levels. The results showed that fixation duration first hovered around chance levels and then showed a sharp rise immediately prior to reaching the criterion. The shape of the learning curve resembled the similarly discontinuous curves obtained with older children, suggesting that infants also selected stimulus features through an active testing process.

However, these results cannot be taken as being conclusive because the infants were trained in a fixed-trials procedure rather than with a learning criterion. In the fixed-trials procedure, all infants were given a set number of training trials, which allows infants to vary in their final level of learning at the end of the training phase. Consequently, the learning curve was derived from criteria constructed on a post hoc rather than a prospective basis. The present experiment was designed to avoid this problem by training all infants to an a priori criterion.

Our second objective was to identify which stimulus components are most likely to be selected by infants and how selection of components—indexed by attention preferences—might relate to the speed of solving the discrimination problem. As suggested by the consistent increase of fixation on a stimulus feature during the learning phase, results from the experiments reported thus far have shown that infants learn to discriminate stimuli on the basis of particular stimulus dimensions; moreover, whenever preferences were analyzed, infants were observed to prefer particular forms and particular colors (the forms of the plus sign and the circle and the colors blue and red). These results, however, do not tell us whether infants may prefer to attend to the dimension of color or to that of form. Color has been noted to be preferred over form by children younger than approximately 4 years of age (Spears, 1964, 1966; Suchman & Trabasso, 1966a, 1966b; Wright & Vlietstra, 1975), but this differential dominance is not entirely reliable during infancy (Brian & Goodenough, 1929). The preference seen at older ages may be due to experience (Gaines, 1970); however, there have been more recent arguments that preferences for particular dimensions emerge as a function of maturation (Zeaman & Hanley, 1983).

If infants do have preferences for a component, their ability to learn discriminations should be facilitated. Attention theory holds that children who are unable to focus attention on the relevant dimension will find learning the discrimination difficult if not impossible; this prediction has been supported by findings that, prior to attainment of the solution, long runs of trials in which responding remains at chance levels characterize the performance of developmentally or cognitively delayed subjects (House & Zeaman, 1960; Zeaman, 1978; Zeaman & House, 1967). By contrast, children who are able to locate the relevant dimension attentionally should learn faster (House & Zeaman, 1960; Zeaman & House, 1963), and, if that dimension is also a preferred or dominant one, learning should occur very quickly.

In the present experiment, one stimulus compound comprising two dimensions was made relevant (e.g., a green triangle); moreover, these particular features were made redundant for the solution of a discrimination-learning task—that is, infants could select either dimension feature in order to solve the problem. For example, the selection of either the color green or the triangle form would lead to problem solution. The prediction here was that, whichever dimension infants select as dominant, they should show relatively rapid attainment of the learning criterion. For infants without a preferred dimension, learning should be commensurately slower. These possibilities may be tested by observing the relation between speed of learning the discrimination and dimension dominance.

Method

Subjects

Twenty-eight 9-month-olds (17 males and 11 females) composed the final sample; four additional infants were tested but excluded owing to fussiness ($N = 3$) or failure to learn the discrimination after extended training ($N = 1$; see below). The sample was predominantly Caucasian, healthy, and without known developmental abnormalities. More detailed characteristics of the sample are reported in Table 7.

Apparatus and Stimuli

The apparatus was identical to that used in the previously reported experiments. Only one pair of stimuli—a green triangle and a blue circle—was used in all trials. These were presented to the left and right of the infant's midline; neither stimulus appeared in the same position for more than two consecutive trials. Half the subjects were trained to fixate on the green triangle and the other half on the blue circle; the side on which the reinforced target first appeared was balanced across the groups.

Design and Procedure

Because the same stimulus was reinforced over the entire training period, both features in the compound (i.e., both the color and the shape of the figure) were relevant for correctly solving the problem; this method is called the *redundant relevant cues task* (Trabasso & Bower, 1968; Zeaman & Hanley, 1983). Thus, the information attended to could vary among infants;

TABLE 7

SAMPLE CHARACTERISTICS FOR EXPERIMENT 4

	M	SD	Min.	Max.
Infants:				
Testing age (weeks)	39.2	.5	38.6	40.6
Gestational age (weeks)	40.1	1.5	37.0	43.0
Birth weight (grams)	3,538.5	405.3	2,707.4	4,309.2
Mothers:				
Age (years)	31.0	4.4	22.0	42.0
Highest level of education (years)	15.0	1.9	12.0	18.0

selectively attending to color, to form, or to the stimulus as a compound all would lead to success in solving the discrimination.

Training continued until infants met either one of two learning criteria: two consecutive trials in which duration of fixation was 50% longer than the initial fixation on the reinforced target or two consecutive trials in which the mean proportion of fixation duration was above 65%. These criteria were selected by determining the highest mean duration of fixation attained in an earlier study of 3-, 6-, and 9-month-old infants in the synchronous reinforcement paradigm (Colombo, Mitchell, et al., 1990) and on the basis of prior infant conditioning experiments (e.g., Fagen & Ohr, 1990). A minimum of four trials proved necessary to meet the criterion; the maximum number of trials given to an infant was 14. All infants but one met the criterion; the one who did not was not administered the test phase and was dropped from the study.

The test phase was presented following a delay of approximately 4 sec while the slides were reset. In the four test trials, the features of the trained stimulus compound were dissociated: the pairs now consisted of a green circle and a blue triangle, and no reinforcement was given for fixating on either target. Under these conditions, fixation on the color feature indicated that the infant had paid attention to color during the training phase, while fixation on the form feature demonstrated attention to form. Equal proportions of fixation time (50%) devoted to the two stimuli during the test phase indicated either a lack of preference for either feature, or attention to both features, or attention to the training stimulus as a compound.

Results

Data Reduction

The proportions of fixation per trial on the reinforced stimulus were averaged across two successive trials into blocks. We averaged over four adjacent trials in the previous experiments because, with three dimensions (color, form, and position), four trials were needed to obtain a data point for the reinforced feature across which all other features were varied. In this experiment, the redundancy of the reinforced stimulus features across color and form permitted averaging over only two trials, collapsing across variation in the remaining dimension of position.

Preliminary Analyses

A between-subjects MANOVA failed to reveal any effect due to the infants' sex ($F[4, 23] = 1.93$, $p =$ N.S.) on the precriterion, criterion, and test blocks; thus, this factor was excluded from further analyses.

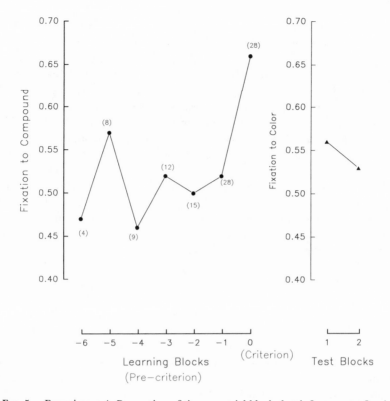

Fig. 5.—Experiment 4: Proportion of time per trial block that infants spent fixating on the relevant stimulus compound as plotted backward from the learning criterion. The number of subjects at each data point is given in parentheses. Also shown is the proportion of time per test block that infants spent fixating on the color dimension following training to determine color vs. form dominance. The chance level (μ) is represented by the dotted line at .50.

Training-Phase Analyses

Backward learning curve.—The mean proportion of fixation duration to the reinforced stimulus compound was plotted *backward* for each infant from the point at which the subject met criterion (Hayes, 1953). As shown in Figure 5, prior to attainment of the criterion, the points on the learning curve hovered at about the chance level of .50. Just as infants attained the criterion, however, the proportion of fixation duration to the reinforced target increased precipitously from .52 to .66. Each of these points was tested against the theoretical mean (μ) of .50. The mean proportion of fixation in the precriterion block of two trials immediately preceding the criterion (which can be considered as analogous to the trial of last error [TLE] as specified in Gholson et al., 1972) proved no greater than μ; however, it became greater than μ at the criterion ($t[27] = 9.12, p < .001$). The mean number of blocks to reach criterion was 3.71 (SD = 1.98).

Preferences for stimulus features.—To test whether learning was affected by which stimulus compound the infant was trained to fixate on (green triangle vs. blue circle) or the side on which the stimuli first appeared (left vs. right), a mixed-model ANOVA was performed across the precriterion and criterion blocks. A significant main effect of blocks ($F[1, 24] = 72.06$, $p < .001$) indicated that duration of fixation increased from the precriterion to the criterion blocks. A main effect was also obtained for the training stimulus compound ($F[1, 24] = 12.29, p < .001$): the blue circle ($M = .65$) was fixated on for an overall longer duration across these two blocks during the learning phase than was the green triangle ($M = .53$). However, a separate ANOVA indicated that neither the nature of the training stimulus nor the position in which it appeared had any effect on the number of blocks that infants took to meet the criterion.

Test-Phase Analyses

Tests for color/form dominance.—Infants' performance in the test phase is also shown in Figure 5. Here, we have plotted the proportion of fixation duration during that phase to the initially trained color dimension to test for dominance of color or form. The rationale for this is explicated in the following example. If the infant was trained to attend to the green triangle and color is a dominant or preferred dimension, then, when the features are dissociated during the test phase (i.e., green circle vs. blue triangle), the infant should continue to expect reinforcement based on the (dominant) color feature and thus fixate on the green stimulus despite the fact that it is presented within the context of a novel form (the circle). By contrast, if form is dominant, then the infant should fixate on the form that had been reinforced during training, and the response should thus be to the triangle, despite the fact that it is presented within the context of a novel color (blue). As plotted in Figure 5, selection of color during the test phase is indicated by fixation duration greater than .50; fixation less than .50 indicated selection of form.

The mean fixation was .56 (SD = .12) on the first test block and .53 (SD = .14) on the second, indicating the selection of color. A test of these fixation proportions against μ yielded a significant difference only for the first test block ($t[27] = 2.53, p < .05$). This finding of color dominance supports the previous predictions that color dominance should developmentally precede form dominance (Zeaman & Hanley, 1983) and extends the applicability of this progression to infancy (Brian & Goodenough, 1929; Spears, 1964, 1966; Suchman & Trabasso, 1966a).

Tests for other training-phase effects.—A separate ANOVA was run to test for effects over test blocks due to the stimulus on which the infant was trained and to initial side of presentation. No significant main or interaction effects emerged for either of these factors. Thus, infants' performance during the test phase was unaffected by these procedural differences during the training phase.

Individual Differences:
Tests for Effects of Speed of Learning

To examine whether infants' speed of learning was related to a preference for the dimension of color, correlations were calculated between the number of blocks to criterion and percentage fixation on color on the first and second test blocks. The number of blocks to criterion was negatively related to percentage fixation on color on the first test block at a statistically significant level ($r = -.43, p < .05$); although the correlation for the second test block was in the same direction, it was not statistically significant ($r = -.20, p =$ N.S.). Thus, faster learning during the initial training was associated with attention to color during the first test block.

Because this observed correlation established a relation between number of blocks to criterion and fixation on the color dimension, the next step was to examine more precisely whether dominance for the color dimension was related to individual differences among infants in their learning performance. To do this, the number of trial blocks to criterion was split at the median of three blocks to divide the sample into fast learners (infants who learned in two blocks [$N = 13$]) and slow learners (those who learned in three or more blocks [$N = 15$]) (see Table 8). A mixed-model ANOVA involving factors of learning speed (fast vs. slow) and test block (2) was conducted on proportions of the fixation on the trained color feature. A

TABLE 8

SPEED OF LEARNING BY DIMENSION DOMINANCE

	FIXATION ON COLOR DIMENSION[a]	
NUMBER OF BLOCKS TO CRITERION	Test Block 1	Test Block 2
Two ($N = 13$)	.61[b]	.56
	(.09)	(.14)
Three or more ($N = 15$) ..	.51	.49
	(.13)	(.14)

[a] Standard deviations are presented in parentheses.
[b] Significantly different from μ ($t[12] = 4.49, p < .001$).

51

main effect was found for learning speed ($F[1, 26] = 5.01$, $p < .05$); fast learners showed color dominance across both blocks of the test phase ($M = .59$), while slow learners did not show any kind of preference across the test blocks ($M = .50$). There was no significant difference between the two groups in mean proportions of fixation across the test blocks.

Discussion

The first notable finding that resulted from this experiment was the discontinuity of the learning curve that we obtained. This curve replicates both the shape and the extent of levels of fixation obtained by Colombo, Mitchell, et al. (1990). Moreover, because in the present experiment infants were trained to a criterion instead of using a fixed trial procedure, individual differences in learning performance are more clearly indicated, such as the chance-level nature of responding prior to criterion.

This experiment also supported the predictions that Zeaman and House's attention theory makes concerning the relation between attention and learning. Infants who learned the discrimination fastest also showed a preference for the color dimension during the test phase, supporting the proposition that speed of learning a discrimination is related to the subject's facility at locating the relevant dimension. It is plausible to conclude that infants who took longer to solve the discrimination failed to select any particular dimension during the initial learning phase. Moreover, this conclusion is independent of which stimulus was trained: while the blue circle was fixated on at a higher level than the green triangle, this preference did not affect the number of trials to learn the criterion or preference for a dimension during the test phase.

Unfortunately, this experiment cannot be used to determine whether slow learners who failed to select either dimension during the test phase learned the original stimulus as a compound. Were it so, both stimuli shown in the test phase would be new, and the infant would not have any basis on which to select either. Moreover, it is also possible that infants who were slow to learn actually learned both components of the original stimulus and consequently selected both stimulus features during the test phase; this, of course, would result in responding to both stimuli to an equal degree.

Furthermore, it is plausible that some infants entered the experiment with an established preference for selecting a particular dimension and that this acted to facilitate learning and was manifested during the test phase (House & Zeaman, 1960; Suchman & Trabasso, 1966b; Zeaman & House, 1963, 1967). We cannot determine whether the selective attention exhibited during the test phase was a preexisting preference because dominance was assessed only after the training phase; we did so because assessment of preferences prior to training has been noted to influence the selection of dimensions during later performance (Tighe, Tighe, Waterhouse, & Vasta, 1970). In any event, it is not necessary that infants have a preference for some dimension at the outset in order for learning to be facilitated; it is possible that some of them are simply able to hone in more quickly on the stimuli relevant to solving the problem (Zeaman, 1978).

Regardless of how slow learners attend to the training compound or whether a dimension is preferred from the outset or isolated by the infant throughout training, the conclusion that fast learning is closely associated with attention selection of a dimension continues to hold.

V. GENERAL DISCUSSION: IMPLICATIONS FOR THE DEVELOPMENT OF ATTENTION AND LEARNING

The experiments reported in this *Monograph* constitute the first programmatic exploration of discrimination learning in preverbal human subjects. The intent of this work was to further our understanding of the processes by which preverbal infants acquire information and solve the problems that they encounter in everyday life situations; the discrimination-learning paradigm makes it possible to examine how infants' well-documented abilities to discriminate and recognize visual stimuli operate in dynamic learning situations. A further motivation for these studies was to examine specific hypotheses derived from long-held models of older children's discrimination learning. The recent development of the synchronous reinforcement technology (Colombo, Mitchell, et al., 1990; Mitchell, 1990; see also Tyrrell, Minard, & Wass, 1992; Tyrrell, Zingaro, & Minard, 1992) made it possible to extend the developmental predictions specified by these models to preverbal, infant ages. In the discussion that follows, the major findings of our experiments are considered within the context of their theoretical significance for understanding the development of learning and attention as well as the relation between these two areas. The findings have implications for several broad areas of inquiry into the development of attention and learning, and the discussion is organized around those topics.

SELECTIVE ATTENTION IN INFORMATION ACQUISITION

The first major finding of the studies that we have reported is that 9-month-olds selectively attend to, and respond on the basis of, a single feature embedded in a compound stimulus (Broadbent, 1971; Enns & Cameron, 1987; Neill, 1977; Posner, Snyder, & Davidson, 1980; Treisman, 1982; Well et al., 1980). This ability to select relevant and important stimulus properties within an array of varying inputs is one of the most fundamental skills in information processing (Bruner et al., 1956).

It has been shown previously that infants even younger than 9 months of age are capable of discriminating components of stimuli within the context of more complex stimulus compounds. For example, Cohen (Cohen, 1973; Cohen & Gelber, 1975; Cohen et al., 1971) demonstrated that 4-month-olds are sensitive to changes of color and of form components of a compound visual stimulus as well as to changes in the compound as a whole (see also Cornell & Strauss, 1973; Fagan, 1977). The unique contribution of the present findings is that infants were shown to learn to attend selectively to and respond on the basis of a single relevant stimulus component embedded among other irrelevant and varying stimulus features (see also Fagen, 1980).

Future research on this general topic might be designed to test various developmental predictions about the disruption that irrelevant stimuli may have on attention to a particular feature (Enns & Girgus, 1985; Lane & Pearson, 1982; Navon & Gopher, 1979). Although in the set of tasks that we gave them infants did learn the discriminations quite easily, and although the presence of irrelevant stimulus features did not obviously impede their performance, comparisons with other age groups tested under similar conditions will be necessary to confirm the conclusion that we are advancing.

WHOLE VERSUS COMPONENT PROCESSING

The finding that infants can discriminate component features of stimuli and attend to them also bears directly on predictions concerning proposed developmental transitions in the processing of stimuli as wholes versus as components of the whole (e.g., Werner, 1948). It has been theorized that developmentally immature (Garner, 1983; Garner & Felfoldy, 1970; Shepp, 1978, 1983) or perceptually inexperienced (Gibson & Gibson, 1955) organisms are more likely to perceive stimuli as wholes; only as subjects become able to differentiate the stimuli perceptually can selective attention to a dimension or a feature be utilized (Offenbach, 1983; Offenbach & Blumberg, 1985; Shepp, 1983; Shepp & Swartz, 1976).

This general distinction in how stimuli are processed appears in various forms across different literatures, such as compound versus component (House, 1979; Smith, 1979, 1984, 1989; Tighe & Tighe, 1966; Tighe, 1973; Tighe et al., 1971; Tighe & Tighe, 1967; Tighe & Tighe, 1978; Zeaman & Hanley, 1983; Zeaman & House, 1974), integral versus separable analysis (Garner, 1983; Garner & Felfoldy, 1970; Shepp, 1978, 1983; Smith, 1979, 1984, 1989), and global versus local processing (Navon, 1977, 1990; Treisman, 1990; Treisman & Gelade, 1980). Support for the proposed developmental progression from whole to part processing has been well documented in findings that preschoolers and kindergarten-aged children have difficulty responding to components of stimuli (House, 1979; Smith, 1979, 1984, 1989; Tighe & Tighe, 1966; Tighe, 1973; Tighe et al., 1971; Tighe & Tighe, 1967; Tighe & Tighe, 1978; Zeaman & Hanley, 1983).

Our findings that infants are capable of selectively attending to components and dimensions of stimulus compounds appear at odds with the developmental progression of attention and perception seen across preschool-, kindergarten-, and school-aged children. Note, however, that Cohen (1991; Younger, 1990; Younger & Cohen, 1986) has also reported that infants are capable of attending to individual stimulus features in forming perceptual or conceptual categories, suggesting that infants' perceptual mode is synthetic (see also Cohen, 1992).

How is it, then, that, although infants are capable of processing stimulus components, older children appear more likely to respond to stimuli holistically and globally? Pick (1983) has raised the possibility that different processes may be invoked at different ages: both analysis and integration of components may be available from early on in the developmental course, but only during later childhood does the use of differentiation strategies become prevalent. Perception and attention to one portion of the stimulus does not necessarily preclude attention to another portion of the stimulus (Kinchla & Wolfe, 1979); in fact, preschool-aged children are able to perceive both dimensions and features in compounds, even though their preferred perceptual mode of responding tends to be holistic and nonanalytic (Boswell, 1976; Enns & Girgus, 1985; Kemler & Smith, 1978; Lewis, Goldberg, & Campbell, 1969; Stiles, Delis, & Tada, 1991; Ward, 1980).

Considered in this light, our infancy results suggest that the developmental progression in whole-to-part processing may be attributable not to an age-related facility in differentiation but rather to an age-related disposition to choose a particular type among the available processing strategies. Although the sequence and preferred mode of visual processing in infants are not as yet fully determined, further support for our position comes from recent work that establishes the presence of both global and local levels of analysis at 4 months of age (e.g., Colombo, Mitchell, Coldren, & Freeseman, 1991; Freeseman, Colombo, & Coldren, 1993).

DIMENSION PROCESSING

In addition to addressing issues of selective attention to particular stimulus components, our findings are also relevant to the processing of higher-order dimensions of stimuli (i.e., abstracting the dimensions of color and form). Because infants consistently showed better transfer of learning under R and ID shift conditions than under NR or ED conditions, it may be inferred that they were solving the discrimination task by means of dimension processing. That is, the data indicate that infants not only attended to the stimuli but also responded on the basis of abstract stimulus dimensions (color, form, or position) rather than on the basis of isolated stimulus features. Earlier work by Colombo, McCollam, et al. (1990) had raised the possibility of dimension processing in 10-month-olds, but, to our knowledge, this is the first direct indication that infants are capable of extracting such higher-order stimulus properties and using them in a learning situation. Thus, a major excitement of our results is that they demonstrate the presence of true *concept* learning on the part of 9-month-olds.

ON THE NATURE AND DEVELOPMENT OF MEDIATION

The finding of dimension learning and transfer of such learning in preverbal humans contrasts greatly with the predictions of the Kendler mediation model. Recall that the Kendler model holds that young children (e.g., younger than 5 years of age) solve discrimination-learning problems by attaching response strength to particular stimulus features. Older subjects, on the other hand, are posited to learn in a discontinuous manner that is more consistent with the concept of dimension processing; most likely, this transition in the nature of learning occurs by virtue of older subjects' ability to attach verbal labels to the dimension aspects of the stimulus set. By demonstrating that 9-month-old infants appear to solve discrimination tasks through dimension processing (as inferred from superior transfer of learning on R and ID shift tasks), the present set of experiments clearly does not support this model's prediction for preverbal subjects and stands in stark contrast to much of the evidence on which this model was based. Moreover, our findings generate several conclusions regarding the propensity for dimension processing in humans.

First of all, these findings indicate that verbal mediation is not a necessary condition for dimension processing; that is, it is not necessary for a subject to be able to formulate a verbal rule that guides responding to a particular dimension during a discrimination-learning task. Nine-month-old infants lack language skills, and what receptive skills they do have are not nearly sophisticated enough to contend plausibly that such verbal structures are available to aid them in such learning. The hypothesized operation of *verbal* mediation in dimension processing is thus refuted—however, is it necessary to postulate *any* mediation to account for infants' performance on these discrimination-learning tasks?

We propose that the consistently superior transfer seen on R and ID tasks requires positing involvement of some type of central mediation in 9-month-olds' solution to such learning problems. In order to transfer the solution of the learning task within dimensions across novel features (as they did in, e.g., the ID/ED task in Experiment 3), it seems that the infants would have had to form some representation of the dimension itself that was in some way free of the specific features that compose the dimension. Because the formation and use of such a representation fits the characterization of mediation (e.g., Zeaman & House, 1974), we propose that infants are solving these tasks through mediated albeit nonverbal responding.

The theoretical position most consistent with the concept of a nonverbal mediation process is the attention model proposed by Zeaman and House (1963, 1974). This model predicts that children of all ages will attend to dimensions of stimuli, even though it does not directly specify how quickly attention to dimensions could be learned by very young and preverbal subjects (see, e.g., Dickerson et al., 1972; Zeaman & House, 1974). Moreover, the attention model asserts that a central orienting response (OR) operates in (i.e., mediates) both the R/NR and the ID/ED tasks, although proponents of this model preferred the ID/ED shift task as an index of dimension learning because it eliminates possible lingering effects from responses to the same features across phases (Esposito, 1975; Reese & Lipsitt, 1970; Shepp & Turrisi, 1966; Slamecka, 1968; Wolff, 1967).

In support of the claims of attention theory, some data have been reported showing that even young children can perform both R and ID shift tasks (Campione, 1970; House & Zeaman, 1962). The findings that we have reported are in agreement with these earlier data and consequently suggest that the tenets of the attention model may be applicable to the study of preverbal cognition and cognitive development (as has been profitably done in the past; see Fagan, 1977). Our contention implies that a dimensionally based OR represents a fundamental process that is operative much earlier than has been previously specified, either theoretically or empirically, by the attention model (e.g., Dickerson et al., 1972; House, 1989; Zeaman & House, 1974; cf. Kendler & Kendler, 1966). This proposition is in line with compelling arguments made by others that investigators should focus on when and under what circumstances children mediate, and not just to ask whether children mediate (Cole & Medin, 1973; Gollin & Rosser, 1974). Just how such mediated learning and attention to dimensions may operate during the course of learning by infants even younger than 9 months of age is currently under investigation.

As noted earlier, our findings indicate that the verbal mediation model is incorrect in its account of developmental changes in discrimination-learning performance. There is, however, an apparent contradiction between the present data (which are consistent with adult data in showing

9-month-olds' superiority of transfer in R and ID conditions) and previous data showing that, for preschoolers, transfer of learning is better in NR conditions. The overall age-related pattern of data thus suggests that dimension processing occurs in infants and in older children, that accumulative response-strength learning is employed by young preschoolers, and that a return to dimension-processing strategies characterizes adults.

The shift in strategies from preschoolers to adults had been previously explained in terms of the onset of involvement of the verbal mediation system in learning (Kendler & Kendler, 1962). Since this system has not yet been mastered by very young children, they were presumed to be still learning in the manner specified by Spence (1936). Verbally advanced older children and adults, on the other hand, were presumed to be learning in a manner more akin to discontinuous functioning. Now, however, the present data suggest that the performance of preschoolers may reflect a regression to a less mature type of learning rather than a lower developmental limit of the more mature learning approach.

We propose a revision of the original developmental account that still incorporates the onset of the operation of the verbal system as the reason for this apparent regression in preschoolers' performance. The data suggest that 9-month-olds are capable of solving discrimination-learning tasks via nonverbally mediated dimension processing; this nonverbal mediation system is fairly efficient and functional, and the 9-month-olds use it with facility. For the more complex tasks that will eventually face the child, however, the use of verbal mediation is a clearly superior strategy. The child is thus faced with a need to shift the systems that mediate learning at some point in early childhood. As a result of the increased demands generated by the transition from the use of a nonverbal to a verbal mediation system, it is plausible that the young child may need to relearn the information collected earlier under the rubric of the new system. Once the new system is mastered during later childhood and adulthood, however, learning efficiency is optimized.

We believe that this scenario accounts for the age-related pattern of results. In it, preschoolers are not suffering from a mediation deficit; rather, they are an age group in transition, caught in the midst of changing from one strategy for coding and storage of information input to another. Under such conditions, a return to more primitive, accumulative learning processes (in which the distinction between relevant and irrelevant features is somewhat blurred) and a temporary drop in learning efficiency would actually be expected. The situation can be likened to that of a writer who is learning to produce a document on a new word processor or of a self-trained pianist who is relearning his or her musical repertoire using more efficient fingering patterns. Although the first mediation system is functional (the writer can produce documents on the old word processor, and the pianist can play the repertoire with the less efficient fingering), optimization of efficiency and the quality of the products will be greatly enhanced over the long run with the new and more advantageous system; however, in the interval during which the new system is being installed, learning will most likely be a slower and more accumulative process. We might expect that similar regressions in the choice of learning strategies would occur for any subject in completely novel learning situations where a mediation system does not exist or where the application of an already existing mediation system is not immediately obvious to the learner.

DO INFANTS FORMULATE AND TEST HYPOTHESES?

The final part of this discussion explores the implications of contending that the infant's response in the discriminationlearning paradigm is *mediated.* Psychological constructs like mediation are valuable in allowing investigators to model variables that intervene between the external stimulus and the response (Kendler & Kendler, 1975; Reese, 1977; see also Posner & Shulman, 1979), and the concept of mediation has undergone significant revision since its original application. Although the term is no longer used in the context of modern information-processing theories, several theorists imply that the concept of mediation lives on under the guise of more complex processes that transform behavioral performance through such representations as rules, strategies, or hypotheses (Cantor, 1977; Cantor & Spiker, 1989; Flavell et al., 1966; Reese, 1962, 1977; Reese & Porges, 1976; Spiker, 1989).

Our data suggest that the infants whom we tested were learning to solve these discrimination problems through nonverbally mediated dimension responses. As suggested by models of children's hypothesis testing (Gholson & Schuepfer, 1979; Kendler, 1979a, 1979b, 1981, 1983; Schuepfer & Gholson, 1983), the type of responding observed in the present set of experiments to occur in infants may be paradigmatic of actual hypothesis testing. In other words, we propose that our data indicate that 9-month-olds may be capable of selecting and testing hypotheses in solving these discrimination-learning tasks. For instance, selection of a dimension during learning as a basis for response may occur serially as infants select and test the different dimensions for their outcome (Zeaman, 1978; Zeaman & House, 1963). Further, by saying that these mediated responses are nonverbal, we imply that hypotheses may be formulated and acted on without the aid of a verbal system.

The potential presence of hypotheses in nonverbal organisms has long been recognized and has been a topic for speculation (e.g., Bower, 1989;

Krechevsky, 1932b). The present findings suggest that a hypothesis-testing approach to problem solving may be independent of, and likely precedes, the development of verbal representation in humans.

Along with the data from the first three experiments, this account of learning as an active process was further supported by the backward learning curve obtained in Experiment 4. Infants' learning curves hovered around chance until just before criterion, at which point they rose dramatically to levels indicating solution of the problem. Theoretically, these findings may be interpreted as evidence that infants actively test solutions until the one that is consistently reinforced is discovered (Bower & Trabasso, 1964; Krechevsky, 1932b; Zeaman & House, 1963). A final point in favor of this interpretation is the observation yielded by Experiment 4 that, if the infant has some form of preference for the dimension that is relevant for solving the problem, learning is facilitated.

It is worth noting that Overton and Reese (1981) have pointedly questioned whether descriptive backward learning curves are appropriate for testing an explanatory learning process. This criticism loses some force, however, when one considers that probes of hypothesis-testing learning have determined that children test hypotheses prior to solution that but they do not show the hypothesis to solve the problem correctly prior to meeting the criterion (Gholson et al., 1972). Nevertheless, in order to strengthen any conclusions about whether infants actively select stimuli and operate according to hypothesis-testing systems, we need designs in which probe trials, in which no reinforcement is given, are inserted into the training phase (Levine, 1966). Whether infants adopt hypotheses to achieve task solution would be indicated by a unique pattern of responses over the probe trials; if infants show a pattern of responding that does not correspond to any possible hypothesis, it would suggest that they are responding randomly.

In addition to the present evidence, several other previous findings also suggest that infants may be capable of generating and using simple rules (Siegler, 1991, describes these as "if . . . then" statements). Among these, some examples include findings that infants regulate responding to sequences of events through the formation of expectancies (Fagen, Morrongiello, Rovee-Collier, & Gekowski, 1984; Haith, Hazan, & Goodman, 1988) and transfer responding to a particular relation between pairs of stimuli over several sets of stimuli (Tyrrell, Minard, & Wass, 1992; Tyrrell, Zingaro, & Minard, 1992; Vella & Zeedyk, 1990).

Several investigators of adults' learning have argued that formulation of higher-order units places less demand on limited processing resources than having to remember individual stimuli (Broadbent, 1971; Graham, 1992; Kahneman & Treisman, 1984; Kanwisher & Driver, 1992; Treisman, 1986). Also, studies of inductive learning and transfer in both adults (Holland et al., 1986; Hunt, 1962) and children (Brown, 1978, 1982) indicate that overarching principles may be transferred from a set of facts or observations to serve as a basis for solving future problems. Attending to, or abstracting, higher-order stimulus dimensions may similarly allow infants to better organize and more efficiently represent the relevant stimulus information in learning situations.

SUMMARY

The experiments in this program of research serve several functions. First, they confirm the viability of the synchronous reinforcement procedure as a method for studying the processes and products of learning in infants (see also Colombo, Mitchell, et al., 1990; Mitchell, 1990; Tyrrell, Minard, & Wass, 1992; Tyrrell, Zingaro, & Minard, 1992). Second, the results of these studies clearly demonstrate the presence of a number of important information-processing skills in 9-month-old infants, such as selective attention to relevant information and dimension processing. The findings bear directly on developmental research on whole-part processing and on mediation; specifically, the results demonstrate component processing at an age when processing of compound wholes might be expected to dominate.

More important, however, are the findings concerning dimension processing that were replicated across all the experiments. This evidence indicates that preverbal, 9-month-old infants learn in a manner that was previously associated only with highly verbal subjects and thus suggests the need for the revision of long-standing accounts of how children solve such learning problems. We have offered an alternate account of the developmental change in dimension processing that is consistent with the data but that reconceptualizes the qualitative differences seen in the learning of preschoolers as being the effect of a transition in mediating systems rather than a deficit in mediation itself.

Perhaps the most provocative implication of these findings is the suggestion that, in learning discrimination tasks such as were used in our experiments, infants select stimulus dimensions and make responses based on these choices. This pattern of behavior strongly suggests that infants may be cognitively capable of hypothesis testing; whether infants do, in fact, generate and test hypotheses while attempting to solve discrimination-learning problems remains to be tested directly. If preverbal infants are indeed capable of testing hypotheses in the course of problem solving, this would place them squarely on a plane with older children and adults (e.g., Siegler, 1991). If one accepts this possibility, its further implication is that such a hypothesis-testing approach to problem solving is independent of verbal skill or representation; thus, linguistic representations may be mapped onto already-existing perceptual-cognitive skills that form the basis for hypothesis testing rather than contributing directly to their development.

Finally, it is hoped that the present studies illustrate the value of seeking to explicate the processes underlying the cognitive products that are so well and widely documented in the human infant. For the past two decades, research in the field of infancy has focused on the theme of *competence*, establishing that the human infant is much more proficient than once believed, and showing that, in fact, infants possess fairly sophisticated cognitive and perceptual skills (Horowitz & Colombo, 1990). Beyond establishing the existence of such competencies, we hope that the studies that we have reported in this *Monograph* provide a first step toward understanding how these competencies are attained and executed.

REFERENCES

Amsel, A. (1989). *Behaviorism, neobehaviorism, and cognitivism in learning theory: Historical and contemporary perspectives.* Hillsdale, NJ: Erlbaum.

Banks, M. S., & Salapatek, P. (1983). Infant visual perception. In M. M. Haith & J. J. Campos (Eds.), P. H. Mussen (Series Ed.), *Handbook of child psychology: Vol. 2. Infancy and developmental psychobiology.* New York: Wiley.

Barkley, R. A. (1989). Attention deficit–hyperactivity disorder. In E. J. Mash & R. A. Barkley (Eds.), *Treatment of childhood disorders.* New York: Guilford.

Berlyne, D. (1958). The influence of albedo and complexity on visual fixation in the human infant. *British Journal of Psychology,* **56,** 315–318.

Bickel, W. K., Stella, M. E., & Etzel, B. C. (1984). A reevaluation of stimulus overselectivity: Restricted stimulus control or stimulus control hierarchies. *Journal of Autism and Developmental Disorders,* **14**(2), 137–157.

Boff, R. B., Kaufman, L., & Thomas, J. P. (Eds.). (1986). *Handbook of perception and human performance: Vol. 2. Cognitive processes and performance.* New York: Wiley.

Bornstein, M. H. (1984). A descriptive taxonomy of psychological categories used by infants. In C. Sophian (Ed.), *Origins of cognitive skills.* Hillsdale, NJ: Erlbaum.

Boswell, S. L. (1976). Young children's processing of asymmetrical and symmetrical patterns. *Journal of Experimental Child Psychology,* **22,** 309–318.

Bower, G. H., & Trabasso, T. (1964). Concept identification. In R. C. Atkinson (Ed.), *Studies in mathematical psychology.* Stanford, Calif.: Stanford University Press.

Bower, T. G. R. (1964). Discrimination of depth in premotor infants. *Psychonomic Science,* **1,** 368.

Bower, T. G. R. (1989). *The rational infant: Learning in infancy.* New York: Freeman.

Brian, C. R., & Goodenough, F. L. (1929). The relative potency of color and form perception at various ages. *Journal of Experimental Psychology,* **12,** 197–213.

Broadbent, D. E. (1958). *Perception and communication.* London: Pergamon.

Broadbent, D. E. (1971). *Decision and stress.* New York: Academic.

Brown, A. L. (1978). Knowing when, where, and how to remember: A problem of metacognition. In R. Glaser (Ed.), *Advances in instructional psychology* (Vol. 1). Hillsdale, NJ: Erlbaum.

Brown, A. (1982). Learning and development: The problems of compatibility, access, and induction. *Human Development,* **25,** 89–115.

Bruner, J. S., Goodnow, J. J., & Austin, G. A. (1956). *A study in thinking.* New York: Wiley.

Buss, A. H. (1953). Rigidity as a function of reversal and nonreversal shifts in the learning of successive discriminations. *Journal of Experimental Psychology,* **45**(2), 75–81.

Buss, A. H. (1956). Reversal and nonreversal shifts in concept formation with partial reinforcement eliminated. *Journal of Experimental Psychology*, **52**(3), 162–166.

Campione, J. C. (1970). Optional intradimensional and extradimensional shifts in children as a function of age. *Journal of Experimental Psychology*, **84**, 296–300.

Campione, J., Hyman, L., & Zeaman, D. (1965). Dimensional shifts and reversals in retardate discrimination learning. *Journal of Experimental Child Psychology*, **2**, 255–263.

Cantor, J. H. (1977). Behavioristic perspectives on a dialectical model of discriminative learning and transfer. In N. Datan & H. W. Reese (Eds.), *Life-span developmental psychology: Dialectical perspectives on experimental research*. New York: Academic.

Cantor, J. H., & Spiker, C. (1989). Children's learning revisited: The contemporary scope of the modified Spence discrimination theory. In H. W. Reese (Ed.), *Advances in child development and behavior* (Vol. **21**). New York: Academic.

Caron, A. J. (1969). Discrimination shifts in three-year-olds as a function of dimensional salience. *Developmental Psychology*, **1**, 333–339.

Caron, A. J. (1970). Discrimination shifts in three-year-olds as a function of shift procedure. *Developmental Psychology*, **3**, 236–241.

Caron, R. F., & Caron, A. J. (1978). Effects of ecologically relevant manipulations on infant discrimination learning. *Infant Behavior and Development*, **1**, 291–307.

Cohen, L. B. (1973). A two-process model of infant visual attention. *Merrill-Palmer Quarterly*, **19**, 157–180.

Cohen, L. B. (1991). Infant attention: An information processing approach. In M. J. Saloman-Weiss & P. R. Zelazo (Eds.), *Newborn attention: Biological constraints and the influence of experience*. Norwood, NJ: Ablex.

Cohen, L. B. (1992). *The myth of differentiation*. Symposium paper presented at the International Conference on Infant Studies, Miami.

Cohen, L. B., DeLoache, J. S., & Strauss, M. S. (1979). Infant visual perception. In J. D. Osofsky (Ed.), *Handbook of infant development*. New York: Wiley.

Cohen, L. B., & Gelber, E. R. (1975). Infant visual memory. In L. B. Cohen & P. Salapatek (Eds.), *Infant perception: From sensation to cognition: Vol. 1. Basic visual processes*. New York: Academic.

Cohen, L. B., Gelber, E. R., & Lazar, M. (1971). Infant habituation and generalization to differing degrees of stimulus novelty. *Journal of Experimental Child Psychology*, **11**, 379–389.

Cohen, L. B., & Salapatek, P. (Eds.). (1975). *Infant perception: From sensation to cognition: Vol. 1. Basic visual processes*. New York: Academic.

Cole, M. (1973). A developmental study of factors influencing discrimination transfer. *Journal of Experimental Child Psychology*, **16**, 126–147.

Cole, M., & Medin, D. (1973). On the existence and occurrence of mediation in discrimination transfer: A critical note. *Journal of Experimental Child Psychology*, **15**, 352–355.

Colombo, J., & Bundy, R. (1981). A method for the measurement of infant auditory selectivity. *Infant Behavior and Development*, **4**, 219–223.

Colombo, J., & Bundy, R. (1983). Infant response to auditory familiarity and novelty. *Infant Behavior and Development*, **6**, 305–311.

Colombo, J., McCollam, K., Coldren, J. T., Mitchell, D. W., & Rash, S. J. (1990). Form categorization in 10-month-olds. *Journal of Experimental Child Psychology*, **49**, 173–188.

Colombo, J., Mitchell, D. W., Coldren, J. T., & Atwater, J. (1990). Discrimination learning during the first year: Stimulus and positional cues. *Journal of Experimental Psychology: Learning, Memory, and Cognition*, **16**(1), 98–109.

Colombo, J., Mitchell, D. W., Coldren, J. T., & Freeseman, L. J. (1991). Individual differences in infant attention: Are short lookers faster processors or feature processors? *Child Development*, **62**, 1247–1257.

Colombo, J., O'Brien, M., Mitchell, D. W., Roberts, K., & Horowitz, F. D. (1987). A lower boundary for category formation in preverbal infants. *Journal of Child Language*, **14**, 383–385.

Cornell, E. H., & Strauss, M. S. (1973). Infants' responsiveness to compounds of habituated visual stimuli. *Developmental Psychology*, **9**, 73–78.

Dickerson, D. J. (1966). Performance of preschool children on three discrimination shifts. *Psychonomic Science*, **4**, 417–418.

Dickerson, D. J., Novik, N., & Gould, S. A. (1972). Acquisition and extinction rates as determinants of age changes in discrimination shift behavior. *Journal of Experimental Psychology*, **95**(1), 116–122.

Dickerson, D. J., Wagner, J. F., & Campione, J. (1970). Discrimination shift performance of kindergarten children as a function of variation of the irrelevant shift dimension. *Developmental Psychology*, **3**(2), 229–235.

Eimas, P. D. (1965). Comment: Comparisons of reversal and nonreversal shifts. *Psychonomic Science*, **3**, 445–446.

Eimas, P. D. (1966). Effects of overtraining and age on intradimensional and extradimensional shifts in children. *Journal of Experimental Child Psychology*, **3**, 348–355.

Eimas, P. D. (1967). Optional shift behavior in children as a function of overtraining, irrelevant stimuli, and age. *Journal of Experimental Child Psychology*, **5**, 332–340.

Enns, J. T., & Cameron, S. (1987). Selective attention in young children: The relations between visual search, filtering, and priming. *Journal of Experimental Child Psychology*, **44**, 38–63.

Enns, J. T., & Girgus, J. S. (1985). Developmental changes in selection and integrative visual attention. *Journal of Experimental Child Psychology*, **40**, 319–337.

Esposito, N. J. (1975). Review of discrimination shift learning in young children. *Psychological Bulletin*, **82**(3), 432–455.

Estes, W. K. (1960). Learning theory and the new "mental chemistry." *Psychological Review*, **67**, 207–223.

Fagan, J. F. (1977). An attention model of infant recognition. *Child Development*, **48**, 345–359.

Fagan, J. F., & McGrath, S. (1981). Infant recognition memory and later intelligence. *Intelligence*, **5**, 121–130.

Fagen, J. W. (1977). Interproblem learning in ten-month-old infants. *Child Development*, **48**, 786–796.

Fagen, J. W. (1980). Stimulus preference, reinforcer effectiveness, and relational responding in infants. *Child Development*, **51**, 372–378.

Fagen, J. W., Morrongiello, B. A., Rovee-Collier, C., & Gekowski, M. (1984). Expectancies and memory retrieval in three-month-old infants. *Child Development*, **55**, 936–943.

Fagen, J. W., & Ohr, P. S. (1990). Individual differences in infant conditioning and memory. In J. Colombo & J. W. Fagen (Eds.), *Individual differences in infancy*. Hillsdale, NJ: Erlbaum.

Fantz, R. L. (1958). Pattern vision in young infants. *Psychological Review*, **8**, 43–47.

Fantz, R. L. (1961). The origin of form perception. *Scientific American*, **204**, 66–72.

Fantz, R. L. (1964). Visual experience in infants: Decreased attention to familiar patterns relative to novel ones. *Science*, **146**, 668–670.

Fenson, L., Zeedyk, S., & Vella, D. (1990). *How not knowing "how" keeps infants from demonstrating what they know*. Paper presented at the International Conference on Infant Studies, Montreal.

Flavell, J. H., Beach, D. H., & Chinsky, J. M. (1966). Spontaneous verbal rehearsal in a memory task as a function of age. *Child Development*, **37**, 283–299.

Freeseman, L. J., Colombo, J., & Coldren, J. T. (1993). Individual differences in infant visual attention: Four-month-olds' discrimination and generalization of global and local stimulus properties. *Child Development, 64,* 1191–1203.

Gaines, R. (1970). Children's selective attention to stimuli: Set or stage? *Child Development, 41,* 970–991.

Garner, W. R. (1983). Asymmetric interactions of stimulus dimensions in perceptual information processing. In T. J. Tighe & B. E. Shepp (Eds.), *Perception, cognition, and development: Interactional analyses.* Hillsdale, NJ: Erlbaum.

Garner, W. R., & Felfoldy, G. L. (1970). Integrality of stimulus dimensions in various types of information processing. *Cognitive Psychology, 1,* 225–241.

Gholson, B. (1980). *The cognitive-developmental basis of human learning.* New York: Academic.

Gholson, B., & Beilin, H. (1979). A developmental model of human learning. In H. W. Reese (Ed.), *Advances in child development and behavior* (Vol. **13**). New York: Academic.

Gholson, B., Dattell, A. R., Morgan, D., & Eymard, L. A. (1989). Problem-solving, recall, and mapping relations in isomorphic transfer and nonisomorphic transfer among preschoolers and elementary school children. *Child Development, 60,* 1172–1187.

Gholson, B., Levine, M., & Phillips, S. (1972). Hypotheses, strategies, and stereotypes in discrimination learning. *Journal of Experimental Child Psychology, 13,* 423–446.

Gholson, B., & Rosenthal, T. L. (Eds.). (1984). *Applications of cognitive-developmental theory.* Orlando, FL: Academic.

Gholson, B., & Schuepfer, T. (1979). Commentary on Kendler's paper: An alternative perspective. In H. W. Reese (Ed.), *Advances in child development and behavior* (Vol. **13**). New York: Academic.

Gibson, J. J., & Gibson, E. J. (1955). Perceptual learning: Differentiation or enrichment? *Psychological Review, 62,* 32–41.

Glaser, R. (1981). The future of testing: A research agenda for cognitive psychology and psychometrics. *American Psychologist, 36,* 923–936.

Glaser, R. (1990). The reemergence of learning theory within instructional research. *American Psychologist, 45*(1), 29–39.

Gollin, E. S., & Rosser, M. (1974). On mediation. *Journal of Experimental Child Psychology, 17,* 539–544.

Graham, F. K., Ernhart, C. B., Craft, M., & Berman, P. W. (1964). Learning of relative and absolute size concepts in preschool children. *Journal of Experimental Child Psychology, 1,* 26–36.

Graham, N. (1992). Breaking the visual stimuli into parts. *Current Directions in Psychological Science, 1*(2), 55–61.

Greeno, J. (1980). Psychology of learning, 1960–1980: One participant's observations. *American Psychologist, 35*(8), 713–728.

Haith, M. M. (1990). Progress in the understanding of sensory and perceptual processes in early infancy. *Merrill-Palmer Quarterly, 36*(1), 1–26.

Haith, M. M., Hazan, C., & Goodman, G. S. (1988). Expectation and anticipation of dynamic visual events by 3.5-month-old babies. *Child Development, 59,* 467–479.

Hayes, K. L. (1953). The backward curve: A method for the study of learning. *Psychological Review, 60,* 269–275.

Hill, S. D. (1965). The performance of young children on three discrimination learning tasks. *Child Development, 36,* 425–435.

Holland, J. H., Holyoak, K. J., Nisbett, R. E., & Thagard, P. R. (1986). *Induction: Processes of inference, learning, and discovery.* Cambridge, MA: MIT Press.

Horowitz, F. D. (1968). Infant learning and development: Retrospect and prospect. *Merrill-Palmer Quarterly, 14,* 101–120.

Horowitz, F. D. (1969). Learning, development, and individual differences. In L. P. Lipsitt

& H. W. Reese (Eds.), *Advances in child development and behavior* (Vol. **4**). New York: Academic.

Horowitz, F. D. (1974). Visual attention, auditory stimulation, and language discrimination in young infants. *Monographs of the Society of Research in Child Development,* **39**(5–6, Serial No. 158).

Horowitz, F. D., & Colombo, J. (1990). Future agendas and directions in infancy research. *Merrill-Palmer Quarterly,* **36**(1), 173–178.

House, B. J. (1979). Attention to components or compounds as a factor in discrimination transfer performance. *Journal of Experimental Child Psychology,* **27**, 321–331.

House, B. J. (1989). Some current issues in children's selective attention. In H. W. Reese (Ed.), *Advances in child development and behavior* (Vol. **21**). New York: Academic.

House, B. J., & Zeaman, D. (1960). Visual discrimination learning and intelligence in defectives of low mental age. *American Journal of Mental Deficiency,* **65**, 51–58.

House, B. J., & Zeaman, D. (1962). Reversal and nonreversal shifts in discrimination learning in retardates. *Journal of Experimental Psychology,* **63**, 444–451.

Hunt, E. B. (1962). *Concept learning: An information-processing approach.* New York: Wiley.

Hunt, J. McV. (1961). *Intelligence and experience.* New York: Ronald.

Husaim, J. S., & Cohen, L. B. (1981). Infant learning of ill-defined categories. *Merrill-Palmer Quarterly,* **27**(4), 443–456.

Kahneman, D., & Treisman, A. (1984). Changing views of attention and automaticity. In R. Parasuraman & D. R. Davies (Eds.), *Varieties of attention.* New York: Academic.

Kanwisher, N., & Driver, J. (1992). Objects, attributes, and visual attention: Which, what, and where. *Current Directions in Psychological Science,* **1**(1), 26–31.

Kelleher, R. T. (1956). Discrimination learning as a function of reversal and nonreversal shifts. *Journal of Experimental Psychology,* **51**, 379–384.

Kemler, D. G., & Smith, L. B. (1978). Is there a developmental trend from integrality to separability in perception. *Journal of Experimental Child Psychology,* **26**, 498–507.

Kendler, H. H., & D'Amato, M. (1955). A comparison of reversal and nonreversal shifts in human concept formation behavior. *Journal of Experimental Psychology,* **49**, 165–174.

Kendler, H. H., Glasman, L. D., & Ward, J. W. (1972). Verbal-labeling and cue-training in reversal-shift behavior. *Journal of Experimental Child Psychology,* **13**, 195–209.

Kendler, H. H., Glucksberg, S., & Keston, R. (1961). Perception and mediation in concept learning. *Journal of Experimental Psychology,* **61**(2), 186–191.

Kendler, H. H., & Kendler, T. S. (1962). Vertical and horizontal processes in problem solving. *Psychological Review,* **69**(1), 1–16.

Kendler, H. H., & Kendler, T. S. (1966). Selective attention versus mediation: Some comments on Mackintosh's analysis of two-stage models of discrimination learning. *Psychological Bulletin,* **66**(4), 282–288.

Kendler, H. H., & Kendler, T. S. (1968). Mediation and conceptual behavior. In K. W. Spence & J. T. Spence (Eds.), *The psychology of learning and motivation.* New York: Academic.

Kendler, H. H., & Kendler, T. S. (1975). From discrimination learning to cognitive development: A neobehavioristic odyssey. In W. K. Estes (Ed.), *Handbook of learning and cognitive processes: Vol. 1. Introduction to concepts and issues.* Hillsdale, NJ: Erlbaum.

Kendler, T. S. (1960). Learning, development, and thinking. *Annals of the New York Academy of Sciences,* **91**, 52–63.

Kendler, T. S. (1963). Development of mediating responses in children. In J. C. Wright & J. Kagan (Eds.), *Basic cognitive processes in children. Monographs of the Society for Research in Child Development,* **28**(2, Serial No. 86).

Kendler, T. S. (1972). An ontogeny of mediational deficiency. *Child Development,* **43**, 1–17.

Kendler, T. S. (1974). The effect of training and stimulus variables on reversal-shift ontogeny. *Journal of Experimental Child Psychology*, **17**, 87–106.

Kendler, T. S. (1979a). The development of discrimination learning: A levels-of-functioning explanation. In H. W. Reese & L. P. Lipsitt (Eds.), *Advances in child development and behavior* (Vol. **13**). New York: Academic.

Kendler, T. S. (1979b). Reply to commentaries. In H. W. Reese & L. P. Lipsitt (Eds.), *Advances in child development and behavior* (Vol. **13**). New York: Academic.

Kendler, T. S. (1981). Development of discrimination learning and problem-solving: A critical review of "The cognitive-developmental basis of human learning: Studies in hypothesis-testing." *Developmental Review*, **1**(2), 146–162.

Kendler, T. S. (1983). Labeling, overtraining, and levels of functioning. In T. J. Tighe & B. E. Shepp (Ed.), *Perception, cognition, and development: Interactional analyses*. Hillsdale, NJ: Erlbaum.

Kendler, T. S., & Kendler, H. H. (1959). Reversal and nonreversal shifts in kindergarten children. *Journal of Experimental Psychology*, **58**, 56–60.

Kendler, T. S., Kendler, H. H., & Learnard, B. (1962). Mediated responses to size and brightness as a function of age. *American Journal of Psychology*, **75**, 571–586.

Kendler, T. S., Kendler, H. H., & Wells, D. (1960). Reversal and nonreversal shifts in nursery school children. *Journal of Comparative and Physiological Psychology*, **53**, 83–88.

Keppel, G. (1991). *Design and analysis: A researcher's handbook* (3d ed.). Englewood Cliffs, NJ: Prentice-Hall.

Kessen, W. (1963). Research in the psychological development of infants: An overview. *Merrill-Palmer Quarterly*, **9**, 83–94.

Kinchla, R. A., & Wolfe, J. M. (1979). The order of visual processing: Top-down, bottom-up, or middle-out. *Perception and Psychophysics*, **25**(3), 225–231.

Krechevsky I. (1932a). The genesis of "hypotheses" in rats. *University of California Publications in Psychology*, **6**(4), 45–64.

Krechevsky, I. (1932b). "Hypothesis" versus "chance" in the pre-solution period in sensory discrimination learning. *University of California Publications in Psychology*, **6**(3), 27–44.

Krechevsky, I. (1933). The docile nature of "hypotheses." *Journal of Comparative Psychology*, **15**, 429–441.

Krechevsky, I. (1938). A study of the continuity of the problem-solving process. *Psychological Review*, **45**, 107–133.

Lane, D. M., & Pearson, D. A. (1982). The development of selective attention. *Merrill-Palmer Quarterly*, **28**(3), 317–337.

Lashley, K. S. (1929). *Brain mechanisms and intelligence: A quantitative study of injuries to the brain.* Chicago: University of Chicago Press.

Levine, M. (1966). Hypothesis behavior by humans during discrimination learning. *Journal of Experimental Psychology*, **71**, 331–338.

Levine, M. (1975). *A cognitive theory of learning.* Hillsdale, NJ: Erlbaum.

Lewis, M., Goldberg, S., & Campbell, H. (1969). A developmental study of information processing within the first three years of life: Response decrement to a redundant signal. *Monographs of the Society for Research in Child Development*, **34**(9, Serial No. 133).

Linder, B. A., & Siegel, L. S. (1983). The learning paradigm as a technique for investigating cognitive development. In J. Bisanz, G. L. Bisanz, & R. Kail (Eds.), *Learning in children.* New York: Springer.

Lipsitt, L. P. (1963). Learning in the first year of life. In L. P. Lipsitt & C. C. Spiker (Eds.), *Advances in child development and behavior* (Vol. **1**). New York: Academic.

Lipsitt, L. P. (1966). Learning processes of human newborns. *Merrill-Palmer Quarterly*, **12**(1), 45–71.

McCall, R. B. (1975). Attention in the infant: Avenue to the study of cognitive development. In D. Walcher & D. L. Peters (Eds.), *Early childhood: The development of self-regulatory mechanisms.* New York: Academic.

McKirdy, L. S., & Rovee, C. K. (1978). The reinforcing efficacy of visual and auditory components in infant conjugate conditioning. *Journal of Experimental Child Psychology,* **25,** 80–89.

Millar, W. S. (1972). A study of operant conditioning under delayed reinforcement in early infancy. *Monographs of the Society for Research in Child Development,* **37**(2, Serial No. 147).

Mitchell, D. W. (1988). *Process and product: The assessment of individual differences in the psychometric and cognitive traditions.* Unpublished manuscript, University of Kansas, Department of Human Development.

Mitchell, D. W. (1990). *Fixation time as a predictor of 3- and 4-month-old infants' cognitive performance.* Unpublished doctoral dissertation, University of Kansas, Department of Human Development.

Mumbauer, C. C., & Odom, R. C. (1967). Variables affecting the performance of preschool children in intradimensional, reversal, and extradimensional shifts. *Journal of Experimental Psychology,* **75,** 180–187.

Navon, D. (1977). Forest before trees: The precedence of global features in visual perception. *Cognitive Psychology,* **9,** 353–363.

Navon, D. (1990). Does attention serve to integrate features? *Psychological Review,* **97**(3), 453–459.

Navon, D., & Gopher, D. (1979). On the economy of the human processing system. *Psychological Review,* **86,** 214–255.

Neill, W. T. (1977). Inhibitory and facilitatory processes in selective attention. *Journal of Experimental Psychology: Human Perception and Performance,* **3,** 444–450.

Offenbach, S. I. (1979). Effect of cue salience on discrimination learning. *Bulletin of the Psychonomic Society,* **14**(12), 129–130.

Offenbach, S. I. (1983). The concept of dimension in research in children's learning. *Monographs of the Society for Research in Child Development,* **48**(6, Serial No. 204).

Offenbach, S. I., & Blumberg, F. C. (1985). The concept of dimensions in developmental research. *Advances in child development and behavior* (Vol. **19**). New York: Academic.

Olson, G., & Sherman, T. S. (1983). Attention, learning, and memory in infants. In M. M. Haith & J. J. Campos (Eds.), P. H. Mussen (Series Ed.), *Handbook of child psychology: Vol. 2. Infancy and developmental biology.* New York: Wiley.

Overton, W. F., & Reese, H. W. (1981). Conceptual prerequisites for an understanding of stability-change and continuity-discontinuity. *International Journal of Behavioral Development,* **4,** 99–123.

Papousek, H. (1967). Conditioning during early postnatal development. In Y. Brackbill & G. G. Thompson (Eds.), *Behavior in infancy and early childhood: A book of readings.* New York: Free Press.

Pick, H. L. (1983). Some issues on the relation between perceptual and cognitive development. In T. J. Tighe & B. E. Shepp (Eds.), *Perception, cognition, and development: Interactional analyses.* Hillsdale, NJ: Erlbaum.

Posner, M. I., & Shulman, G. L. (1979). Cognitive science. In E. Hearst (Ed.), *The first century of experimental psychology.* Hillsdale, NJ: Erlbaum.

Posner, M. I., Snyder, C. R., & Davidson, B. J. (1980). Attention and the detection of signals. *Journal of Experimental Psychology: General,* **109,** 160–174.

Ramey, C., Hieger, R., & Klisz, T. (1972). Synchronous reinforcement of vocal responses in failure to thrive infants. *Child Development,* **43,** 1449–1455.

Reese, H. W. (1962). Verbal mediation as a function of age level. *Psychological Bulletin,* **59,** 502–509.

Reese, H. W. (1977). Discrimination learning and transfer: Dialectical perspectives. In N. Datan & H. W. Reese (Eds.), *Life-span developmental psychology: Dialectical perspectives on experimental research.* New York: Academic.

Reese, H. W., & Lipsitt, L. P. (1970). *Experimental child psychology.* New York: Academic.

Reese, H. W., & Porges, S. W. (1976). Development of learning processes. In V. Hamilton & M. D. Vernon (Eds.), *The development of cognitive processes.* New York: Academic.

Restle, F. (1960). Note on the "hypothesis" theory of discrimination learning. *Psychological Reports, 7,* 194.

Rock, I. (1957). The role of repetition in associative learning. *American Journal of Psychology, 70,* 186–193.

Rose, S. A., & Feldman, J. (1990). Infant cognition: Individual differences and developmental continuities. In J. Colombo & J. F. Fagen (Eds.), *Individual differences in infancy.* Hillsdale, NJ: Erlbaum.

Rovee, C., & Rovee, D. (1969). Conjugate reinforcement of infant exploratory behavior. *Journal of Experimental Child Psychology, 8,* 33–39.

Rovee-Collier, C. (1987). Learning and memory in infancy. In J. D. Osofsky (Ed.), *Handbook of infant development* (2d ed.). New York: Wiley.

Rovee-Collier, C., & Capatides, J. B. (1979). Positive behavioral contrast in 3-month-old infants on multiple conjugate reinforcement schedules. *Journal of the Experimental Analysis of Behavior, 32,* 15–27.

Rovee-Collier, C., & Fagen, J. W. (1981). The retrieval of memory in early infancy. In L. P. Lipsitt (Ed.), *Advances in infancy research* (Vol. 1). Norwood, NJ: Ablex.

Rovee-Collier, C. K., & Gekowski, M. J. (1979). The economics of infancy: A review of conjugate reinforcement. In H. W. Reese & L. P. Lipsitt (Eds.), *Advances in child development and behavior* (Vol. 13). New York: Academic.

Rust, K. J., & Kendler, T. S. (1987). Lower level encoding: Holistic or nonselective? *Developmental Review, 7,* 326–362.

Sameroff, A. J., & Cavanaugh, P. J. (1979). Learning in infancy: A developmental perspective. In J. D. Osofsky (Ed.), *Handbook of infant development.* New York: Wiley.

Schreibman, L. (1975). Effects of within-stimulus and extra-stimulus prompting on discrimination learning in autistic children. *Journal of Applied Behavior Analysis, 8,* 91–112.

Schuepfer, T., & Gholson, B. (1983). From response-set to prediction hypotheses: Rule acquisition among preschoolers and second graders. *Journal of Experimental Child Psychology, 36,* 18–31.

Sears, R. R. (1975). Your ancients revisited: A history of child development. In E. M. Hetherington (Ed.), *Reviews of research in child development* (Vol. 5). Chicago: University of Chicago Press.

Shepp, B. E. (1978). From perceived similarity to dimensional structure: A new hypothesis about perceptual development. In E. Rosch & B. B. Lloyd (Eds.), *Cognition and categorization.* Hillsdale, NJ: Erlbaum.

Shepp, B. E. (1983). The analyzability of multidimensional objects: Some constraints on perceived structure, the development of perceived structure, and attention. In T. J. Tighe & B. E. Shepp (Eds.), *Perception, cognition, and development: Interactional analyses.* Hillsdale, NJ: Erlbaum.

Shepp, B. E., & Swartz, K. B. (1976). Selective attention and the processing of integral and nonintegral dimensions. *Journal of Experimental Child Psychology, 22,* 73–85.

Shepp, B. E., & Turrisi, F. D. (1966). Learning and transfer of mediating responses in discriminative learning. In N. R. Ellis (Ed.), *International review of research in mental retardation* (Vol. 2). New York: Academic.

Siegler, R. (1983). Information-processing approaches to development. In W. Kessen

(Ed.), P. H. Mussen (Series Ed.), *Handbook of child psychology: Vol. 1. History, theory, and methods.* New York: Wiley.

Siegler, R. S. (1991). *Children's thinking* (2d ed.). Englewood Cliffs, NJ: Prentice-Hall.

Simmons, M. W. (1964). Operant discrimination learning in human infants. *Child Development,* **35,** 737–748.

Simmons, M. W., & Lipsitt, L. P. (1961). An operant-discrimination apparatus for infants. *Journal of the Experimental Analysis of Behavior,* **4,** 233–235.

Siqueland, E. R. (1964). Operant conditioning of head turning in four-month-old infants. *Psychonomic Science,* **1,** 223–224.

Siqueland, E. R., & Lipsitt, L. P. (1966). Conditioned head-turning in human newborns. *Journal of Experimental Child Psychology,* **3,** 356–376.

Slamecka, N. J. (1968). A methodological analysis of shift paradigms in human discrimination learning. *Psychological Bulletin,* **69**(6), 423–438.

Smiley, S. S., & Weir, M. W. (1966). Role of dimensional dominance in reversal and nonreversal shift behavior. *Journal of Experimental Child Psychology,* **4,** 296–307.

Smith, L. B. (1979). Perceptual development and category generalization. *Child Development,* **50,** 705–715.

Smith, L. B. (1984). Young children's understanding of attributes and dimensions: A comparison of conceptual and linguistic measures. *Child Development,* **55,** 363–380.

Smith, L. B. (1989). A model of perceptual classification in children and adults. *Psychological Review,* **96**(1), 125–144.

Sokolov, E. (1963). *Perception and the conditioned reflex.* New York: Macmillan.

Sophian, C. (1980). Habituation is not enough: Novelty preferences, search, and memory in infancy. *Merrill-Palmer Quarterly,* **26,** 239–257.

Spears, W. C. (1964). Assessment of visual preference and discrimination in the four month old infant. *Journal of Comparative and Physiological Psychology,* **57,** 381–386.

Spears, W. C. (1966). Visual preference in the four month old infant. *Psychonomic Science,* **4,** 237–238.

Spence, K. W. (1936). The nature of discrimination learning in animals. *Psychological Review,* **47,** 271–288.

Spence, K. W. (1937a). Analysis of the formation of visual discrimination habits in chimpanzees. *Journal of Comparative Psychology,* **23,** 77–100.

Spence, K. W. (1937b). The differential response in animals to stimuli varying within a single dimension. *Psychological Review,* **44,** 430–444.

Spence, K. W. (1938). Gradual versus sudden solution of discrimination problems by chimpanzees. *Journal of Comparative Psychology,* **25,** 213–224.

Spence, K. W. (1940). Continuous versus non-continuous interpretations of discrimination learning. *Psychological Review,* **47,** 271–288.

Spence, K. W. (1956). *Behavior theory and conditioning.* New Haven, CT: Yale University Press.

Spence, K. W. (1960). Conceptual models of spatial and non-spatial selective learning. In K. W. Spence (Ed.), *Behavior theory and learning: Selected papers.* Englewood Cliffs, NJ: Prentice-Hall.

Spiker, C. C. (1989). Cognitive psychology: Mentalistic or behavioristic. In H. W. Reese (Ed.), *Advances in child development and behavior* (Vol. **21**). New York: Academic.

Spiker, C. C., & Cantor, J. H. (1983). Components in the hypothesis-testing strategies of young children. In T. J. Tighe & B. E. Shepp (Eds.), *Perception, cognition, and development: Interactional analyses.* Hillsdale, NJ: Erlbaum.

Stevenson, H. (1970). Learning in children. In P. H. Mussen (Ed.), *Carmichael's manual of child psychology.* New York: Wiley.

Stevenson, H. (1972). *Children's learning*. Englewood Cliffs, NJ: Prentice-Hall.

Stevenson, H. (1983). How children learn: The quest for a theory. In W. Kessen (Ed.), P. H. Mussen (Series Ed.), *Handbook of child psychology: Vol. 1. History, theory, and methods*. New York: Wiley.

Stiles, J., Delis, D. C., & Tada, W. L. (1991). Global-local processing in preschool children. *Child Development, 62,* 1258–1275.

Stone, L. J., Smith, H. T., & Murphy, L. B. (1973). *The competent infant: Research and commentary*. New York: Basic.

Suchman, R. G., & Trabasso, T. (1966a). Color and form preferences in young children. *Journal of Experimental Child Psychology, 3,* 177–187.

Suchman, R. G., & Trabasso, T. (1966b). Stimulus preferences and cue function in young children's concept attainment. *Journal of Experimental Child Psychology, 3,* 188–198.

Tighe, L. S. (1965). Effect of perceptual pretraining on reversal and nonreversal shifts. *Journal of Experimental Psychology, 70*(4), 379–385.

Tighe, L. S., & Tighe, T. J. (1966). Discrimination learning: Two views in historical perspective. *Psychological Bulletin, 66*(5), 353–370.

Tighe, L. S., & Tighe, T. J. (1969). Transfer from perceptual pretraining as a function of number of task dimensions. *Journal of Experimental Child Psychology, 8,* 494–502.

Tighe, L. S., Tighe, T. J., Waterhouse, M. D., & Vasta, R. (1970). Dimensional preference and discrimination shift learning in children. *Child Development, 41,* 737–746.

Tighe, T. J. (1973). Subproblem analysis of discrimination learning. In G. H. Bower (Ed.), *The psychology of learning and motivation* (Vol. 7). New York: Academic.

Tighe, T. J., Glick, J., & Cole, M. (1971). Subproblem analysis of discrimination-shift learning. *Psychonomic Society, 24*(4), 159–160.

Tighe, T. J., & Tighe, L. S. (1965). Reply to Eimas. *Psychonomic Science, 3,* 446.

Tighe, T. J., & Tighe, L. S. (1967). Discrimination shift performance as a function of age and shift procedure. *Journal of Experimental Psychology, 74*(4), 466–470.

Tighe, T. J., & Tighe, L. S. (1978). A perceptual view of cognitive development. In R. D. Walk & H. Pick (Eds.), *Perception and experience*. New York: Plenum.

Tighe, T. J., & Tighe, L. S. (1987). A failure to differentiate. *Developmental Review, 7,* 363–369.

Trabasso, T., & Bower, G. H. (1968). *Attention in learning: Theory and research*. New York: Wiley.

Treisman, A. (1982). Perceptual grouping and attention in visual search for features and for objects. *Journal of Experimental Psychology: Human Perception and Performance, 8,* 194–214.

Treisman, A. (1986). Properties, parts, and objects. In K. R. Boff, L. Kaufman, & J. P. Thomas (Eds.), *Handbook of perception and human performance: Vol. 2. Cognitive processes and performance*. New York: Wiley.

Treisman, A. (1990). Variations on the theme of feature integration: Reply to Navon (1990). *Psychological Review, 97*(3), 460–463.

Treisman, A., & Gelade, G. A. (1980). A feature integration theory of attention. *Cognitive Psychology, 12,* 97–136.

Tyrrell, D. J., Minard, K. L., & Wass, T. S. (1992). *Generalized match-to-sample learning in human infants*. Poster presented at the International Conference of Infancy Studies, Miami.

Tyrrell, D. J., Zingaro, M. C., & Minard, K. L. (1992). *Learning and transfer of identity/ difference relationships by infants*. Poster presented at the International Conference of Infancy Studies, Miami.

Underwood, B. J. (1975). Individual differences as a crucible in theory construction. *American Psychologist, 30,* 128-134.

Vella, D., & Zeedyk, M. S. (1990). *Conceptual problem solving at age two years.* Poster presented at the International Conference on Infant Studies, Montreal.

Ward, T. B. (1980). Separable and integral responding by adults and children to the dimensions of length and density. *Child Development, 51,* 52–56.

Watson, J. S. (1966). The development and generalization of "contingency analysis" in early infancy: Some hypotheses. *Merrill-Palmer Quarterly, 12,* 123–135.

Watson, J. S. (1967). Memory and "contingency analysis" in infant learning. *Merrill-Palmer Quarterly, 13,* 55–76.

Watson, J. S. (1969). Operant conditioning of visual fixation in infants under visual and auditory reinforcement. *Developmental Psychology, 1,* 508–516.

Weisberg, P., & Simmons, M. W. (1966). A modified WGTA for infants in their second year of life. *Journal of Psychology, 63,* 99–104.

Well, A. D., Lorch, E. P., & Anderson, D. R. (1980). Developmental trends in distractibility: Is absolute or proportional decrement the appropriate measure of interference? *Journal of Experimental Child Psychology, 30,* 109–124.

Werner, H. (1948). *Comparative psychology of mental development.* New York: International Universities Press.

White, S. H. (1970). The learning theory tradition and child psychology. In P. H. Mussen (Ed.), *Carmichael's manual of child psychology.* New York: Wiley.

Wolff, J. L. (1967). Concept-shift and discrimination-reversal learning in humans. *Psychological Bulletin, 68*(6), 369–408.

Wright, J. C., & Vlietstra, A. G. (1975). The development of selective attention: From perceptual exploration to logical search. In H. W. Reese (Ed.), *Advances in child development and behavior.* New York: Academic.

Wyckoff, B. (1952). The role of observing responses in discrimination learning. *Psychological Review, 59,* 431–442.

Younger, B. A. (1990). Infant categorization: Memory for category-level and specific item information. *Journal of Experimental Child Psychology, 50,* 131–155.

Younger, B. A., & Cohen, L. B. (1986). Developmental change in infant's perception of correlations among attributes. *Child Development, 57,* 803–815.

Zeaman, D. (1978). Some relations of general intelligence and selective attention. *Intelligence, 2,* 55–73.

Zeaman, D., & Hanley, P. (1983). Stimulus preferences as structural features. In T. J. Tighe & B. E. Shepp (Eds.), *Perception, cognition, and development: Interactional analyses.* Hillsdale, NJ: Erlbaum.

Zeaman, D., & House, B. J. (1963). An attentional theory of retardate discrimination learning. In N. R. Ellis (Ed.), *Handbook of mental deficiency.* New York: McGraw-Hill.

Zeaman, D., & House, B. J. (1967). The relation of IQ and learning. In R. M. Gagne (Ed.), *Learning and individual differences.* Columbus, OH: Merrill.

Zeaman, D., & House, B. J. (1974). Interpretations of developmental trends in discriminative transfer effects. In A. D. Pick (Ed.), *Minnesota symposium on child psychology* (Vol. 8). Minneapolis: University of Minnesota Press.

Zeaman, D., & House, B. J. (1979). A review of attention theory. In N. R. Ellis (Ed.), *Handbook of mental deficiency, psychological theory, and research.* Hillsdale, NJ: Erlbaum.

ACKNOWLEDGMENTS

This report was based on a Ph.D. dissertation conducted by Jeffrey T. Coldren at the Department of Human Development of the University of Kansas. Portions of these data have been presented at meetings of the Society for Research in Child Development in Kansas City (1989) and Seattle (1991) and at the International Conference of Infant Studies in Montreal (1990).

During this work, Jeffrey Coldren was supported by a National Institutes of Health predoctoral traineeship awarded to the Department of Human Development of the University of Kansas (HD07173), grants to John Colombo (federal grants MH14326 and MH43246, March of Dimes Grant 12-89, University of Kansas Biomedical Research Support, and funds from the University of Kansas Mental Retardation Research Center), and a postdoctoral fellowship funded by an Academic Challenge Grant from the State of Ohio to the Department of Psychology of the University of Toledo.

We are grateful for the support of the many families of Johnson County, Kansas, who generously participated in our research and also to Dr. Mary D. Cohen and the staff of the University of Kansas Regents Center for their cooperation and assistance. Thanks to Frances Degen Horowitz, John C. Wright, D. Wayne Mitchell, and Robert A. Haaf for their valuable contributions to this project.

Please address correspondence to Jeffrey T. Coldren, Department of Psychology, Youngstown State University, Youngstown, OH 44555.

COMMENTARY

COGNITIVE PROCESSES EXPLAIN LEARNING ACROSS THE LIFE SPAN: INFANTS AND TODDLERS ARE PEOPLE TOO

Barry Gholson

The program of research that Jeffrey T. Coldren and John Colombo report here addresses fundamental issues in human learning, issues that have fueled ongoing controversy among theorists for nearly a century, essentially since experimental psychology was emerging as an independent scientific discipline in North America (cf. Dewey, 1896; Judd, 1908; Thorndike, 1898, 1899; Thorndike & Woodworth, 1901). The issues are fundamental because they concern whether the basic mechanisms of human knowledge acquisition involve passive conditioning or active cognitive processes. Is learning best conceptualized in terms of conditioning processes that involve the gradual strengthening of associations between specific features of the environment (stimuli) and of specific behaviors (responses)? Alternatively, is it more accurate to conceptualize learning as involving cognitive mechanisms, such as selectively abstracting information, formulating expectancies, and generating rule-governed behavior?

Although there remain a few loose ends, the ingenious experiments and theoretical analyses presented in this *Monograph* have, I believe, provided what most readers will consider the coup de grâce that conclusively resolves the issue in favor of cognitive processes. In my Commentary, I first explore a few specific historical episodes in which the issues were raised and redressed, first in favor of conditioning theory, then, in one instance after another, in favor of cognitive processes. I subsequently highlight some important findings from the current *Monograph* and explore their implications. In my concluding comments, I argue that the few remaining loose ends are really consequences of imprecise experimental methodologies.

The theoretical controversy has its historical roots in nineteenth-century psychology. The formulation addressed by Coldren and Colombo, however, in which the issues were presented precisely enough to be addressed experimentally, did not take shape until much later. Thus, the selective account presented here will be restricted to episodes in this more recent history. In this context, the issues were first joined in research with rats during (roughly) the 1930s (e.g., Krechevsky, 1932, 1933; Lashley, 1929; Spence, 1936, 1937; Tolman, 1932). During the 1940s, the heyday of conditioning theory, the controversy was quiescent. It then reemerged in research with nonhuman primates in the 1950s (Harlow, 1949, 1950; Harlow & Hicks, 1957; Levine, 1959), in research with college students in about 1960 (e.g., Bower & Trabasso, 1963; Bruner, Goodnow, & Austin, 1956; Estes, 1960; Levine, 1963, 1966, 1975; Restle, 1962, 1965; Trabasso & Bower, 1968), and in research with children older than about 5 years of age in the 1970s (Caron, 1970; Cole & Medin, 1973; Eimas, 1969; Gholson, 1980; Gholson & Beilin, 1979; Gholson, Levine, & Phillips, 1972; Gollin & Rosser, 1974; Kendler & Kendler, 1962; Kendler, 1979, 1981, 1983; Reese, 1964; White, 1965, 1970).

As is well known, conditioning theory was firmly established in the mainstream of experimental psychology by the late 1920s. And, if the cognitive challenge to that mainstream position can be said to have a beginning, it probably started with some musings by Lashley (1929) in his classic work on neuropsychology. In a series of studies concerning the effects of brain ablation on learning processes in rats, Lashley included research involving simultaneous brightness discriminations. The rats were required to learn to choose a path leading to either a bright circle or a dark circle in order to obtain food on each trial.

In his description of this research, Lashley (1929) reported that "responses to position, to alternation, or to cues from the experimenter's movements usually preceded the reaction to the light and represent attempted solutions which are within the rat's customary range of activity" (p. 135). He went on to point out that the practice preceding formation of the correct association and any errors that followed that formation were actually irrelevant to the acquisition of the correct response. He described these systematic response patterns that appeared prior to the criterion series as "attempted solutions" and indicated that he had no way to record them objectively. He added that "it justifies us in interpreting the discrimination habit as a simple association acquired only after a number of more familiar solutions have been tried unsuccessfully" (Lashley, 1929, p. 136; see also Levine, 1975, pp. 3–31).

Lashley himself had little more to say on the issue. Krechevsky, however, at the time a graduate student working with Tolman, elaborated on Lashley's earlier reflections, studying systematic response patterns exhibited by rats in a variety of learning tasks. In a series of research reports (e.g., Krechevsky, 1932, 1933, 1937; Tolman, 1932), Krechevsky contended that these response patterns reflected organized behavior and constituted the rats' best guesses about the solution. He presented systematic response patterns in the language of cognitive theory, claiming that they reflected rule-governed behavior, or *hypotheses*.

Conditioning theorists were quick to respond to this challenge (as well as to others; see Gholson & Barker, 1985; Kluver, 1933; Kohler, 1938; Levine, 1975) to the fundamental core of their theory. Although many on both sides contributed to the dispute, its temporary resolution in favor of conditioning theory may be illustrated by some of Spence's work (1936, 1937, 1940).

Spence argued that the systematic response patterns to which Krechevsky referred as *hypotheses* were, in fact, nothing more than uninteresting by-products of the animals' previous conditioning histories. Because all behavior was assumed to be the result of conditioning and extinction processes, systematic response patterns were of no intrinsic interest. In one report, for example, Spence (1936) presented a fairly precise mathematical account in which he showed not only how conditioning and extinction processes predicted the occurrence of systematic response patterns but also that conditioning theory could predict which specific response patterns (e.g., position preference, position alternation) would occur and when they would occur during the course of acquisition.

Because neither Krechevsky nor any other proponent of cognitive theory could make such precise predictions, the issue was temporarily resolved in favor of conditioning theory. Other than an occasional experiment (e.g., Bruner & Postman, 1948), the cognitive approach lay moribund for more than two decades.

By the early 1950s, however, two groups of theorists, one conducting research with nonhuman primates, the other largely concerned with learning processes in college students, were poised to resurrect the issue and resolve it in favor of cognitive theory. The first of these began with Harlow's (1949, 1950) demonstration of learning set in monkeys. He presented his animals with a long series of short two-choice problems. Learning set was said to be acquired when the monkey's solution to each new problem was immediate, that is, when feedback from only the response on the first trial of each new problem was needed for a solution to be achieved. Once the learning set was acquired, each animal showed essentially perfect performance on consecutive problems, even though the solution to each was different from the preceding one. This demonstration was a clear challenge to the assumption that learning occurs incrementally through the gradual strengthening and weakening of specific stimulus-response associations.

Harlow also observed, as had Lashley and Krechevsky, that several types of systematic response patterns (e.g., position alternation, stimulus perseveration) dominated the monkeys' behavior prior to the acquisition of learning set. Because they appeared to inhibit learning, he called these systematic response patterns *error factors*. Harlow concluded that it was important to chart the time course of each one during the acquisition of learning set.

Harlow initially identified four error factors. Each occurred in some monkeys, different ones dominating behavior during successive phases of acquisition. Over the next few years, Harlow, his students, and other primate researchers investigated error factors in a variety of learning tasks. There was little continuity, however, from one research report to the next, with different investigators identifying different error factors that were, for the most part, unrelated to each other. Consequently, the research domain had become somewhat chaotic by the late 1950s, when Levine (1959), a graduate student working with Harlow at the time, presented a new theoretical account.

Levine's account permitted a standard mode of measurement and provided a quantitative theory from which the measurement was derived. Levine enlarged the set of systematic response patterns that was measured, redefined how each was identified, and included the response pattern that was exhibited after learning set was acquired (i.e., consistent correct responding by the second trial on each consecutive problem). Because the term *error factor* was not appropriate for the entire class of systematic response patterns, Levine (1959, 1963) dubbed them *hypotheses*. He pointed out that the animals' behavior was rule governed, that each hypothesis was a determinant of a systematic response pattern, that hypotheses reflected the animals' expectancies, and that only a cognitive theory could adequately account for learning processes in nonhuman primates.

A second resolution of the controversy in favor of cognitive theory occurred very quickly. It actually involved the work of a group of conditioning theorists (e.g., Bush & Mosteller, 1955; Estes & Burke, 1953; Restle, 1955) who elaborated contiguity theory (Guthrie, 1935, 1942), or stimulus sampling theory, into what became commonly known as *mathematical learning theory* (e.g., Hilgard & Bower, 1975). These theorists successfully applied their probabilistic versions of conditioning theory to numerous tasks and subject populations, including college students solving complex concept identification problems. Their theory was mathematically cast, rigorous, and clear in its implications. Thus, it set a demanding standard for competitors (e.g., Bourne & Restle, 1959).

Then, in the late 1950s, several developments occurred, mostly among conditioning proponents themselves, that led to the conclusion that conditioning theory failed to provide an adequate account of learning processes in college students. Eventually, these researchers determined that a theory based on cognitive processes was required (e.g., Restle, 1962, 1965). Full expositions of these events are available elsewhere (see, e.g., Gholson, 1980; Hilgard & Bower, 1975; Kintsch, 1977; Levine, 1975), so only a few are identified here.

In 1957, Rock presented strong evidence that, among college students at least, learning was an all-or-none process, as implied by cognitive theory. That is, learning was not an incremental process involving the gradual strengthening of stimulus-response bonds, as was specified by conditioning theory. If learning was not incremental, conditioning assumptions were suspect, no matter how elegant the theories. Thus, Rock's (1957) findings were critically examined by a number of theorists. Estes (1959, 1960), for example, a leading exponent of conditioning theory at the time, investigated the issue in a set of precisely designed experiments, eventually concluding, like Rock, that learning processes in college students required a cognitive account. Estes presented his findings and rejected conditioning theory in 1960. Other mathematical learning theorists quickly followed Estes's example (e.g., Bourne, Guy, Dodd, & Justesen, 1965; Bower, 1962; Restle, 1962, 1965; Trabasso, 1963). By the mid-1960s, cognitive accounts of learning processes in college students dominated mainstream experimental psychology.

Developmental psychologists were, for the most part, unpersuaded. During the 1960s, most of the work concerned with learning processes in children continued to be conducted within the framework of conditioning theory. Much of that research contrasted verbal mediational with attentional accounts of performance (e.g., Kendler & Kendler, 1962; Kendler & Kendler, 1959; Reese, 1962; Zeaman & House, 1963), using variants of reversal and nonreversal shift methodologies. Mediation theorists posited that, like the rat's, the very young child's behavior may be explained by a single stimulus-response association. To account for the older child's behavior, however, two stimulus-response connections must be chained together. The second link was considered to be necessary because the older child's verbal processes become involved in the behavioral sequence, mediating between environmental input and behavioral output. Because these children had learned to mediate the relevant dimension prior to a reversal shift, they were required only to learn to attach the new observable choice response to the mediator in the transfer task. Therefore, it should be learned faster than a nonreversal.

Younger children were said to be mediationally deficient. This is because their verbal processes play no role in learning. While building excitatory potential to the reinforced stimulus cue on the relevant dimension during original learning, they also build inhibitory potential to the unreinforced cue on that dimension. Thus, in the reversal task, it is necessary to overcome both the excitatory and the inhibitory potential before they reach a neutral point that allows the bond to the new stimulus value on the old dimension to be strengthened. Because the two values on the previously irrelevant dimension are both neutral in terms of inhibitory and excitatory potential at the outset of the shift task, the nonreversal is learned faster than the reversal.

Competing conditioning theorists of the day substituted attentional processes for the verbal mediators, and they frequently assumed that these processes operated in lower phylogeny as well as in very young children (Mackintosh, 1962, 1965; Sutherland, 1959, 1963; Tighe & Tighe, 1966, 1969; Wyckoff, 1952; Zeaman & House, 1963). They maintained the conditioning framework, however, for the other link in the stimulus-response chain. Many of these events are described by Coldren and Colombo in this *Monograph,* and I therefore elaborate on them no further here.

After 1970, the scene changed dramatically when researchers introduced experimental procedures that included probes that exposed the specific hypotheses that children exhibited during learning (e.g., Eimas, 1969, 1970; Gholson et al., 1972; Ingalls & Dickerson, 1969; Phillips & Levine, 1975; Rieber, 1969). These experiments revealed that children exhibit complex rule-governed behavior during the entire course of learning. This chronology of events is described in a variety of accessible sources (e.g., Gholson, 1980; Gholson & Barker, 1985; Gholson & Beilin, 1979; Offenbach, 1983; Siegler, 1991; Tumblin & Gholson, 1981), so I only allude to them here.

By the late 1970s, cognitive accounts of learning processes in children older than 5 years of age were commonplace (e.g., Flavell, 1977, 1985; Gholson, 1980; Klahr & Siegler, 1978; Schuepfer & Gholson, 1983; Siegler, 1978, 1986; Wilkening, Becker, & Trabasso, 1980), and some conditioning theorists then altered their earlier positions. Later statements by these theorists (e.g., Cantor & Spiker, 1978; Kendler, 1979, 1983; Reese, 1977; Spiker & Cantor, 1983), for example, abandoned the assumption that learning processes must be explained in terms of conditioning principles in all children. Instead, there were said to be two modes of learning, one involving conditioning, the other based on cognitive processes. Children younger than 5 or 6 years of age were said to learn primarily through conditioning processes, whereas learning in older children and adults involved cognitive processes. That is, older children selectively abstracted information, formulated expectancies, and generated rule-governed behavior.

The Coup de Grâce: Coldren and Colombo

By the early 1980s, then, the mainstream consensus held that a cognitive theory was required to account for learning processes in nonhuman primates, college students, and children older than about 5 years of age. Although there were numerous suggestions that a cognitive account might be required among even younger children (e.g., Colombo & Mitchell, 1990; Fagen, 1977; Fagen & Ohr, 1990; Gholson & Schuepfer, 1979; Rose & Feldman, 1990; Rovee-Collier, 1987), the issue remained unresolved, mainly because the research methodologies needed to settle it were not available.

In their elegant program of research, however, Coldren and Colombo have demonstrated unequivocally that, at least by 9 months of age, infants exhibit performance that requires a theoretical account based on cognitive processes. In their first two experiments, the infants in the reversal shift conditions performed better than those in the nonreversal conditions. The experiments show that infants selectively abstract information in terms of dimensional properties of stimuli and generate expectancies based on those dimensional properties. These findings directly contradict predictions derived from versions of conditioning theory that were explicitly formulated to address the performance of preverbal children (e.g., Cantor & Spiker, 1978; Kendler & Kendler, 1962, 1966, 1975; Kendler, 1963, 1972, 1979; Kendler & Kendler, 1959; Kuenne, 1946; Spence 1936, 1937, 1956; Spiker & Cantor, 1979, 1983).

Experiments 3 and 4 were even more conclusive. First, Coldren and Colombo demonstrated that preverbal infants selectively abstract and process specific stimulus dimensions during original learning. The infants readily transferred these abstracted dimensions to problems composed of new stimulus cues. These preverbal infants did not learn through the gradual accumulation of response strength to individual features of stimuli, as is proposed by various versions of conditioning theory. In their fourth experiment, Coldren and Colombo showed that learning in infants is a discontinuous none-to-all process: preverbal infants exhibit rule-governed behavior that is prototypical to the systematic hypothesis testing observed in older children and adults.

Conclusions: Loose Ends

Some, of course, may claim that, even though a cognitive theory is required to account for learning processes in infants and children older than about 5 years of age, conditioning theory can still somehow be salvaged. Perhaps sometime after their first birthday and before age 5 or 6, children's learning undergoes some dysfunctional transformation that makes their cognitive processes inoperative: they temporarily learn through the gradual strengthening and weakening of associations between specific stimuli and responses. There is some evidence from the various shift tasks that children in this age range may learn nonreversals faster than reversals, and this is taken as support for conditioning theory (e.g., Kendler & Kendler, 1962; Kendler, 1979; Spiker & Cantor, 1979), although other evidence challenges that conclusion (e.g., Offenbach, 1983; Offenbach & Blumberg, 1985).

What I want to suggest is that the claim in favor of conditioning theory is based on findings that resulted from imprecise research methodologies. These methodologies essentially mask underlying processes that are readily revealed by more precise experimental procedures. The more precise procedures involve decomposing the child's behavior into component processes exhibited in the context of positive and negative feedback.

In order to clarify what is meant, consider a two-choice task of the kind used by Coldren and Colombo. It is composed of three dimensions: two involve object cues (color and form), and a third involves position. There are two values on each of the three dimensions. There are two different types of hypotheses that children older than 5 years of age are known to exhibit in these kinds of tasks. *Prediction* hypotheses are sensitive to feedback consequences. That is, if a prediction hypothesis is confirmed, it is retained and continues to serve as a response determinant; but, if it is disconfirmed, it is rejected, and the child selects a new one. *Response-set* hypotheses, however, are not sensitive to feedback consequences; they are retained as response determinants following both positive and negative feedback.

Both types of hypotheses may be described in terms of the response determinants that are exhibited and how they are affected by positive and negative feedback. Consider, for example, a trial on which the child's response is determined by the prediction that "red" is the solution. If feedback is positive, the child maintains the response determinant and may be said to *win-stay* with respect to that particular cue. Following negative feedback, when red is rejected and a new response determinant selected, the child is said to *lose-shift*. Response-set hypotheses may be described in similar terms. Position alternation, for example, involves a sequence of responses in which the child chooses the left side, then the right, then the left, etc., on consecutive trials, independent of the feedback that is presented. This response sequence would be characterized as *win-shift, lose-shift*, with respect to the position cue as a response determinant. Consistent response to an object cue, such as red, regardless of the feedback consequences, would be *win-stay, lose-stay*, with respect to that particular cue. It is possible, then, to characterize children's performance during discrimination learning in terms of win and lose components along with the object and position referents that serve as response determinants.

A considerable amount of research indicates that the various win and lose components associated with object and position cues are acquired separately, at different rates, and possibly over a protracted period of time (e.g., Fagen, 1977; Gholson & Schuepfer, 1979; Harter, 1967; Levinson & Reese, 1967; Schuepfer & Gholson, 1983). That is, prediction hypotheses of the kind needed to solve standard discrimination-learning problems do not emerge "full blown" in the repertoire of the young child. This is because the child is required to combine the win-stay rule with lose-shift and include only simple object cues as response determinants in order to meet task requirements. These components are acquired independently and at different rates.

To illustrate, I briefly describe some results obtained in research in which children as young as 36 months of age received a series of short two-choice problems similar to those used by Coldren and Colombo. In these problems, feedback trials were followed by blank-trial probes (i.e., a series of trials during which no feedback is given). These probes were used to detect the specific stimulus cues that served as response determinants during the entire course of learning (Schuepfer & Gholson, 1983).

Each problem was composed of three dimensions, with two values on each: position (left or right side) and two object cues, such as color (e.g., red or blue) and form (e.g., circle or square). The blank-trial probes were constructed so that each cue corresponded to a unique combination of responses to the left and right sides during each probe. This made it possible to detect consistent responses to each stimulus cue on each dimension, such as red, or left side. The probes also distinguished among the various alternation patterns, such as red, blue, red, etc. or left side, right side, left side, etc. The children received a series of problems each day until a learning criterion was attained. The solution to each problem involved consistent responses to a simple object cue, such as red or square.

The results revealed that the children exhibited response patterns that corresponded to the various stimulus cues in about 95% of their probes for response determinants (chance was 75%). During precriterion problems, 63% of responses were determined by object cue referents and 31% by position referents. About 10% of both object and position responding involved alternation patterns. In the criterion series, simple object cues served as response determinants in 92% of the probes.

The finding of greatest interest for present purposes concerned how feedback affected the referent cues that determined responses during precriterion problems: the extent to which the children shifted from object to position cues as response determinants and vice versa. When responses to object cues (e.g., red) were followed by positive feedback, the same object cue determined the next response sequence only 53% of the time. Thus, win-stay on object cues was weak. The subjects shifted from an object to a position cue 31% of the time. When responses determined by object cues were followed by negative feedback, the children shifted to position cues 40% of the time. Findings were similar when position cues were response determinants: the children shifted from position referents to object referents about 40% of the time, following both positive and negative feedback.

These young children selectively abstracted information and exhibited rule-governed behavior throughout the course of acquisition, but they were required to learn which specific combination of rules and response determinants was needed to meet the demands of the experiment. That combination, of course, involved the consolidation of win-stay, lose-shift, with respect to simple object cues as response determinants. This rather complex rule was not dominant in the children's repertoires at the outset of acquisition. Rather, a variety of component rules were exhibited individually and in various combinations (Schuepfer & Gholson, 1983). Win-stay on object cues was particularly weak at the outset of acquisition, and position cues frequently served as response determinants. Detecting this rule-governed behavior required very precise experimental procedures, much more precise than those used in the various shift tasks from which the evidence was derived that was taken to support conditioning theory.

When viewed in the context of previous research, some of it dating back half a century or more, what was accomplished by the program of research presented in this *Monograph* will lead most readers to a singular conclusion: any comprehensive theory of human development will require a consistent cognitive account across the entire life span, from birth through old age. In accomplishing this, Coldren and Colombo brought together a massive body of diverse research and theory, which they lucidly articulated in a comprehensive package. The text is well written and stimulating, a pleasure to read and think about. As a result of their efforts, Coldren and Colombo have, I believe, conclusively resolved a fundamental issue that has dogged experimental psychology since its inception.

References

Bourne, L. E., Jr., Guy, D. E., Dodd, D. H., & Justesen, D. R. (1965). Concept identification: The effects of varying length and informational components of the intertrial interval. *Journal of Experimental Psychology, 69*, 624–629.

Bourne, L. E., Jr., & Restle, F. (1959). A mathematical theory of concept identification. *Psychological Review, 66*, 278–296.

Bower, G. H. (1962). An associational model for response and training variables in paired-associate learning. *Psychological Review, 69*, 34–53.

Bower, G. H., & Trabasso, T. (1963). Reversals prior to solution in concept identification. *Journal of Experimental Psychology, 66*, 409–418.

Bruner, J. S., Goodnow, J. J., & Austin, G. A. (1956). *A study of thinking.* New York: Wiley.

Bruner, J. S., & Postman, L. (1948). Symbolic value as an organizing factor in perception. *Journal of Social Psychology, 27*, 203–208.

Bush, R. R., & Mosteller, F. (1955). *Stochastic models for learning*. New York: Wiley.

Cantor, J. H., & Spiker, C. C. (1978). The problem-solving strategies of kindergarten and first-grade children during discrimination learning. *Journal of Experimental Child Psychology*, **26**, 341–358.

Caron, A. J. (1970). Discrimination shifts in three-year-olds as a function of shift procedure. *Developmental Psychology*, **3**, 236–241.

Cole, M., & Medin, D. (1973). On the existence and occurrence of mediation in discrimination transfer: A critical note. *Journal of Experimental Child Psychology*, **15**, 352–355.

Colombo, J., & Mitchell, D. W. (1990). Individual differences in early visual attention: Fixation time and information-processing. In J. Colombo & J. W. Fagen (Eds.), *Individual differences in infancy: Reliability, stability, and prediction*. Hillsdale, NJ: Erlbaum.

Dewey, J. (1896). The reflex arc concept in psychology. *Psychological Review*, **3**, 357–370.

Eimas, P. D. (1969). A developmental study of hypothesis behavior and focusing. *Journal of Experimental Child Psychology*, **8**, 160–172.

Eimas, P. D. (1970). Effects of memory aids on hypothesis behavior and focusing in young children and adults. *Journal of Experimental Child Psychology*, **10**, 319–336.

Estes, W. K. (1959). The statistical approach to learning theory. In S. Koch (Ed.), *Psychology: A study of a science* (Vol. **2**). New York: McGraw-Hill.

Estes, W. K. (1960). Learning theory and the new "mental chemistry." *Psychological Review*, **67**, 207–223.

Estes, W. K., & Burke, C. J. (1953). A theory of stimulus variability in learning. *Psychological Review*, **60**, 276–286.

Fagen, J. W. (1977). Interproblem learning in ten-month-old infants. *Child Development*, **48**, 786–796.

Fagen, J. W., & Ohr, P. S. (1990). Individual differences in infant conditioning and memory. In J. Colombo & J. W. Fagen (Eds.), *Individual differences in infancy: Reliability, stability, and prediction*. Hillsdale, N.J.: Erlbaum.

Flavell, J. H. (1977). *Cognitive development*. Englewood Cliffs, NJ: Prentice-Hall.

Flavell, J. H. (1985). *Cognitive development* (2d ed.). Englewood Cliffs, NJ: Prentice-Hall.

Gholson, B. (1980). *The cognitive-developmental basis of human learning: Studies in hypothesis testing*. New York: Academic.

Gholson, B., & Barker, P. (1985). Kuhn, Lakatos, and Laudan: Applications in the history of physics and psychology. *American Psychologist*, **40**, 755–769.

Gholson, B., & Beilin, H. (1979). A developmental model of human learning. In H. W. Reese & L. P. Lipsitt (Eds.), *Advances in child development and behavior* (Vol. **13**). New York: Academic.

Gholson, B., Levine, M., & Phillips, S. (1972). Hypotheses, strategies, and stereotypes in discrimination learning. *Journal of Experimental Child Psychology*, **13**, 105–118.

Gholson, B., & Schuepfer, T. (1979). Commentary on Kendler's paper: An alternative perspective. In H. W. Reese & L. P. Lipsitt (Eds.), *Advances in child development and behavior* (Vol. **13**). New York: Academic.

Gollin, E. S., & Rosser, M. (1974). On mediation. *Journal of Experimental Child Psychology*, **17**, 539–544.

Guthrie, E. R. (1935). *The psychology of learning*. New York: Harper & Row.

Guthrie, E. R. (1942). A theory of learning in terms of stimulus, response, and association. In *The psychology of learning: Part 11. 41st yearbook of the National Society for the Study of Education*. Chicago: University of Chicago Press.

Harlow, H. F. (1949). The formation of learning sets. *Psychological Review*, **56**, 51–65.

Harlow, H. F. (1950). Analysis of discrimination learning by monkeys. *Journal of Experimental Psychology,* **40,** 26–39.

Harlow, H. F., & Hicks, L. H. (1957). Discrimination learning theory: Uniprocess vs. duoprocess. *Psychological Review,* **64,** 104–109.

Harter, S. (1967). Mental age, IQ, and motivational factors in the discrimination learning set performance of normal and retarded children. *Journal of Experimental Child Psychology,* **5,** 123–141.

Hilgard, E. R., & Bower, G. H. (1975). *Theories of learning* (4th ed.). Englewood Cliffs, NJ: Prentice-Hall.

Ingalls, R. P., & Dickerson, D. J. (1969). Development of hypothesis behavior in human concept identification. *Developmental Psychology,* **1,** 707–716.

Judd, C. H. (1908). The relation of special training to general intelligence. *Educational Review,* **36,** 28–42.

Kendler, H. H., & Kendler, T. S. (1962). Vertical and horizontal processes in problem solving. *Psychological Review,* **69,** 1–16.

Kendler, H. H., & Kendler, T. S. (1966). Selective attention versus mediation: Some comments on Mackintosh's analysis of two-stage models of discrimination learning. *Psychological Bulletin,* **66,** 282–288.

Kendler, H. H., & Kendler, T. S. (1975). From discrimination learning to cognitive development: A neobehavioristic odyssey. In W. K. Estes (Ed.), *Handbook of learning and cognitive processes: Vol. 1. Introduction to concepts and issues.* Hillsdale, NJ: Erlbaum.

Kendler, T. S. (1963). Development of mediating responses in children. In J. C. Wright & J. Kagan (Eds.), *Basic cognitive processes in children. Monographs of the Society for Research in Child Development,* **28**(2, Serial No. 86).

Kendler, T. S. (1972). An ontogeny of mediational deficiency. *Child Development,* **43,** 1–17.

Kendler, T. S. (1979). Toward a theory of mediational development. In H. W. Reese & L. P. Lipsitt (Eds.), *Advances in child development and behavior* (Vol. **13**). New York: Academic.

Kendler, T. S. (1981). Development of discrimination learning and problem solving: A critical review of *The cognitive developmental basis of human learning. Developmental Review,* **1,** 146–162.

Kendler, T. S. (1983). Labeling, overtraining, and levels of functioning. In T. J. Tighe & B. E. Shepp (Eds.), *Perception, cognition, and development: Interactional analyses.* Hillsdale, NJ: Erlbaum.

Kendler, T. S., & Kendler, H. H. (1959). Reversal and nonreversal shifts in kindergarten children. *Journal of Experimental Psychology,* **58,** 56–60.

Kintsch, W. (1977). *Memory and cognition.* New York: Wiley.

Klahr, D., & Siegler, R. S. (1978). The representation of children's knowledge. In H. W. Reese & L. P. Lipsitt (Eds.), *Advances in child development and behavior* (Vol. **12**). Hillsdale, NJ: Erlbaum.

Kluver, H. (1933). *Behavior mechanisms in monkeys.* Chicago: University of Chicago Press.

Kohler, W. (1938). Simple structural functions in the chimpanzee and the chicken [Condensed and translated]. In W. E. Ellis (Ed.), *A source book of gestalt psychology.* New York: Harcourt Brace. (Original work published in 1918)

Krechevsky, I. (1932). "Hypotheses" in rats. *Psychological Review,* **39,** 516–532.

Krechevsky, I. (1933). The docile nature of "hypotheses." *Journal of Comparative Psychology,* **15,** 429–443.

Krechevsky, I. (1937). A note concerning "The nature of discrimination learning in animals." *Psychological Review,* **44,** 97–104.

Kuenne, M. R. (1946). Experimental investigation of the relation of language to transposition behavior in young children. *Journal of Experimental Psychology,* **36,** 471–490.

Lashley, K. S. (1929). *Brain mechanisms and intelligence.* Chicago: University of Chicago Press.

Levine, M. (1959). A model of hypothesis behavior in discrimination learning set. *Psychological Review,* **66,** 353–366.

Levine, M. (1963). Mediation processes in humans at the outset of discrimination learning. *Psychological Review,* **70,** 254–276.

Levine, M. (1966). Hypothesis behavior by humans during discrimination learning. *Journal of Experimental Psychology,* **71,** 331–338.

Levine, M. (1975). *A cognitive theory of learning: Research on hypothesis testing.* Hillsdale, NJ: Erlbaum.

Levinson, B., & Reese, H. W. (1967). Patterns of discrimination learning set in preschool children, fifth-graders, college freshmen, and the aged. *Monographs of the Society for Research in Child Development,* **32**(7, Serial No. 115).

Mackintosh, N. J. (1962). The effects of overtraining on a reversal and a nonreversal shift. *Journal of Comparative and Physiological Psychology,* **55,** 555–559.

Mackintosh, N. J. (1965). Selective attention in animal discrimination learning. *Psychological Bulletin,* **64,** 124–150.

Offenbach, S. I. (1983). The concept of dimension in research in children's learning. *Monographs of the Society for Research in Child Development,* **48**(6, Serial No. 204).

Offenbach, S. I., & Blumberg, F. C. (1985). The concept of dimensions in developmental research. In H. W. Reese (Ed.), *Advances in child development and behavior* (Vol. **19**). New York: Academic.

Phillips, S., & Levine, M. (1975). Probing for hypotheses with adults and children: Blank trials and introtacts. *Journal of Experimental Psychology: General,* **104,** 327–354.

Reese, H. W. (1962). Verbal mediation as a function of age level. *Psychological Bulletin,* **59,** 502–509.

Reese, H. W. (1964). Discrimination learning set in rhesus monkeys. *Psychological Bulletin,* **61,** 321–340.

Reese, H. W. (1977). Discriminative learning and transfer: Dialectical perspectives. In N. Datan & H. W. Reese (Eds.), *Dialectical perspectives on experimental research.* New York: Academic.

Restle, F. (1955). A theory of discrimination learning. *Psychological Review,* **62,** 11–19.

Restle, F. (1962). The selection of strategies in cue learning. *Psychological Review,* **69,** 329–343.

Restle, F. (1965). Significance of all-or-none learning. *Psychological Bulletin,* **64,** 313–325.

Rieber, M. (1969). Hypothesis testing in children as a function of age. *Developmental Psychology,* **1,** 389–395.

Rock, I. (1957). The role of repetition in associative learning. *American Journal of Psychology,* **70,** 186–193.

Rose, S., & Feldman, J. F. (1990). Infant cognition: Individual differences and developmental continuities. In J. Colombo & J. W. Fagen (Eds.), *Individual differences in infancy: Reliability, stability, and prediction.* Hillsdale, NJ: Erlbaum.

Rovee-Collier, C. (1987). Learning and memory in infancy. In J. D. Osofsky (Ed.), *Handbook of infant development* (2d ed.). New York: Wiley.

Schuepfer, T., & Gholson, B. (1983). From response-set to prediction hypotheses: Rule acquisition among preschoolers and second graders. *Journal of Experimental Child Psychology,* **36,** 18–31.

Siegler, R. S. (Ed.). (1978). *Children's thinking: What develops?* Hillsdale, NJ: Erlbaum.

Siegler, R. S. (1986). Unities in strategy choices across domains. In M. Perlmutter (Ed.), *Minnesota symposium on child development* (Vol. **19**). Hillsdale, N.J.: Erlbaum.

Siegler, R. S. (1991). *Children's thinking*. (2d ed.). Englewood Cliffs, N.J.: Prentice-Hall.

Spence, K. W. (1936). The nature of discrimination learning in animals. *Psychological Review*, **43**, 427–449.

Spence, K. W. (1937). The differential response in animals to stimuli varying within a single dimension. *Psychological Review*, **44**, 430–444.

Spence, K. W. (1940). Continuous versus noncontinuous interpretations of discrimination learning. *Psychological Review*, **47**, 271–288.

Spence, K. W. (1956). *Behavior theory and conditioning*. New Haven, CT: Yale University Press.

Spiker, C. C., & Cantor, J. H. (1979). The Kendler levels-of-functioning theory: Comments and an alternative schema. In H. W. Reese & L. P. Lipsitt (Eds.), *Advances in child development and behavior* (Vol. **13**). New York: Academic.

Spiker, C. C., & Cantor, J. H. (1983). Components in the hypothesis-testing strategies of young children. In T. J. Tighe & B. E. Shepp (Eds.), *Perception, cognition, and development: Interactional analyses*. Hillsdale, NJ: Erlbaum.

Sutherland, N. S. (1959). Visual discrimination of shape by octopus: Circles and squares and circles and triangles. *Quarterly Journal of Experimental Psychology*, **11**, 24–32.

Sutherland, N. S. (1963). Cat's ability to discriminate oblique rectangles. *Science*, **139**, 209–210.

Thorndike, E. L. (1898). Animal intelligence: An experimental study of the associative processes in animals. *Psychological Review: Monograph Supplements*, **2**(Serial No. 8).

Thorndike, E. L. (1899). The instinctive reactions of young chicks. *Psychological Review*, **6**, 282–291.

Thorndike, E. L., & Woodworth, R. S. (1901). The influence of one mental function upon the efficiency of other functions. *Psychological Review*, **8**, 247–261, 384–395, 553–564.

Tighe, L. S., & Tighe, T. J. (1966). Discrimination learning: Two views in historical perspective. *Psychological Bulletin*, **66**, 353–370.

Tighe, L. S., & Tighe, T. J. (1969). Transfer from perceptual pretraining as a function of number of task dimensions. *Journal of Experimental Child Psychology*, **8**, 494–502.

Tolman, E. C. (1932). *Purposive behavior in animals and men*. New York: Appleton-Century-Crofts.

Trabasso, T. (1963). Stimulus emphasis and all-or-none learning of concept identification. *Journal of Experimental Psychology*, **65**, 395–406.

Trabasso, T., & Bower, G. H. (1968). *Attention in learning: Theory and research*. New York: Wiley.

Tumblin, A., & Gholson, B. (1981). Hypothesis theory and the development of conceptual learning. *Psychological Bulletin*, **90**, 102–124.

White, S. H. (1965). Evidence for a hierarchical arrangement of learning processes. In L. P. Lipsitt & C. C. Spiker (Eds.), *Advances in child development and behavior* (Vol. **2**). New York: Academic.

White, S. H. (1970). The learning theory approach. In P. H. Mussen (Ed.), *Carmichael's manual of child psychology* (3d ed., Vol. **1**). New York: Wiley.

Wilkening, F., Becker, J., & Trabasso, T. (Eds.). (1980). *Information integration by children*. Hillsdale, NJ: Erlbaum.

Wyckoff, L. B. (1952). The role of observing responses in discrimination learning. *Psychological Review*, **59**, 431–442.

Zeaman, D., & House, B. J. (1963). The role of attention in retardate discrimination learning. In N. R. Ellis (Ed.), *Handbook of mental deficiency*. New York: McGraw-Hill.

ON THE DEVELOPMENT OF THE PROCESSES UNDERLYING
LEARNING ACROSS THE LIFE SPAN

Jeffrey T. Coldren and John Colombo

In his incisive Commentary, Barry Gholson has raised some important and fundamental points that bear on future investigation in the area of attention and learning. At the core of Gholson's conclusions is a concern about the precision of the *shift procedure* methodology that has long been employed throughout the history of discrimination learning—as well as in our own experiments.

In Gholson's analysis, the shift procedure is criticized on the grounds that it may not thoroughly elucidate the processes underlying the discrimination learning tasks that it presents to the subject. Gholson is correct in noting that the reversal/nonreversal and intradimensional/extradimensional shift tasks are methodologically ticklish. Indeed, several other investigators have also identified various problems associated with the intricate nature of the task (Eimas, 1965; Kendler & Kendler, 1975; Shepp & Turrisi, 1966; Slamecka, 1968; Wolff, 1967). However, despite its limitations, the shift task allowed enough scientific leverage for an opening series of studies of discrimination learning with nonverbal organisms and the drawing of some preliminary inferences about the processes operating during the performance of the shift.

Our data suggest that the processes that allow infants to solve such discrimination problems are more similar to processes in older children than to those that may be operating in younger, preschool children. This finding points toward a developmental scenario that is more complex than the traditionally accepted early childhood onset of mediational processes;

we may now set aside the traditional question of whether infants employ mediational processes and focus instead on questions concerning the origins and operation of these mediational processes as well as the change in their deployment over the first several years of life (e.g., Cole & Medin, 1973; Gollin & Rosser, 1974).

We agree generally with Gholson's assessment of the shift task and, in particular, the difficulties that it presents for theoretical interpretations of the development of discrimination problem solving. Owing to the limitation in the shift-task approach that allows only a broad conclusion of the occurrence or nonoccurrence of mediational processes, Gholson is correct in stating that the procedure fails to elucidate other possible processes that may be operating in such tasks. The task-related difficulty involved in the developmental interpretation is compounded by the fact that we have attempted to integrate our findings with the extant developmental literature without data for children across the presumed time of transition—the early childhood years. Therefore, the story is by no means complete at this point as efforts are currently under way to investigate the performance of both 4- and 20-month-olds in order to elucidate the development of these processes fully.

Gholson proposes the use of more precise methodologies that decompose children's responses after positive and negative feedback into fine-grained component processes. Essentially, this method involves observing the unique pattern of children's responses obtained as they solve discrimination problems. Gholson's suggestion is well taken and has the potential to make an important contribution to the program of research with infants. Without doubt, the construct of mediation as it is used in the discrimination learning literature is vague, and there is therefore an obvious need to articulate more precisely the distinct nature and deployment of the processes presumed to be operating during mediated and nonmediated task performance. Given our findings that infants actively select and test responses from an array of dimensions and features to solve discrimination problems in a discontinuous process similar to that which occurs in children and adults, more detailed investigations are warranted with infants, with the aim of considering how infants and toddlers actually select among stimuli, especially when stimuli vary over trials, in order to clarify our tentative developmental progression.

In addition, given the implementation of the precise methodology that Gholson suggests, the next challenge for work in this area is to explain the way in which the cognitive components that contribute to discrimination learning change and develop over the early childhood years. We are still left facing an empirical and theoretical vacuum in this literature regarding the development of discrimination problem-solving skills and strategies across a range of ages early in life—that is, between the infancy and the preschool years. As Gholson (1980) notes, his cognitive-developmental theory makes no explicit specification for the performance of infants. However, from the data that he presents with 36-month-olds (Schuepfer & Gholson, 1983), there are promising indications that even very young children are developing and using complex rule-governed behavior. The implication for our interpretation is that such behavior occurs within the presumed time of transition, thus suggesting that cognitive components may be operating that are not detected by the shift task. These findings necessitate the use of feedback and probe trials under various feedback outcomes across the first several years of life. Once these findings become available, a more comprehensive and complete developmental theory may be articulated that takes into consideration both qualitative and quantitative changes in attentional and hypothesis-testing processes that underlie discrimination problem-solving performance.

References

Cole, M., & Medin, D. (1973). On the existence and occurrence of mediation in discrimination transfer: A critical note. *Journal of Experimental Child Psychology, 15,* 352–355.

Eimas, P. D. (1965). Comment: Comparisons of reversal and nonreversal shifts. *Psychonomic Science, 3,* 445–446.

Gholson, B. (1980). *The cognitive-developmental basis of human learning.* New York: Academic.

Gollin, E. S., & Rosser, M. (1974). On mediation. *Journal of Experimental Child Psychology, 17,* 539–544.

Kendler, H. H., & Kendler, T. S. (1975). From discrimination learning to cognitive development: A neobehavioristic odyssey. In W. K. Estes (Ed.), *Handbook of learning and cognitive processes: Vol. 1. Introduction to concepts and issues.* Hillsdale, NJ: Erlbaum.

Schuepfer, T., & Gholson, B. (1983). From response-set to prediction hypotheses: Rule acquisition among preschoolers and second graders. *Journal of Experimental Child Psychology, 36,* 18–31.

Shepp, B. E., & Turrisi, F. D. (1966). Learning and transfer of mediating responses in discriminative learning. In N. R. Ellis (Ed.), *International review of research in mental retardation* (Vol. 2). New York: Academic.

Slamecka, N. J. (1968). A methodological analysis of shift paradigms in human discrimination learning. *Psychological Bulletin, 69*(6), 423–438.

Wolff, J. L. (1967). Concept-shift and discrimination-reversal learning in humans. *Psychological Bulletin, 68*(6), 369–408.

CONTRIBUTORS

Jeffrey T. Coldren (Ph.D. 1992, University of Kansas) is an assistant professor of psychology at Youngstown State University. He completed a postdoctoral fellowship in the Department of Psychology at the University of Toledo. His research interests in cognitive development include the development of attention and problem-solving skills during infancy and early childhood, the identification of fundamental processes of attention in early infancy, and disorders of attention.

John Colombo (Ph.D. 1981, State University of New York at Buffalo) is an associate professor in the Department of Human Development at the University of Kansas, Lawrence. His major research interests involve the development of attention, perception, learning, and memory, with a special focus on early individual differences in these areas and their relation to childhood intellectual function and development status. He has served on the editorial board of *Child Development* and is the author of a number of journal articles. He has coedited *Individual Differences in Infancy* (with Jeffrey Fagen, 1990) and *Infancy Research: A Summative Look and Directions for the Future* (with Frances Horowitz, 1990) and is the author of *Infant Cognition: Predicting Later Intellectual Function* (1993).

Barry Gholson (Ph.D. 1968, University of Iowa) is professor of psychology at the University of Memphis. His research interests include learning and reasoning processes from a developmental perspective, the history of psychology, and the psychology of science.

STATEMENT OF EDITORIAL POLICY

The *Monographs* series is intended as an outlet for major reports of developmental research that generate authoritative new findings and use these to foster a fresh and/or better-integrated perspective on some conceptually significant issue or controversy. Submissions from programmatic research projects are particularly welcome; these may consist of individually or group-authored reports of findings from some single large-scale investigation or of a sequence of experiments centering on some particular question. Multiauthored sets of independent studies that center on the same underlying question can also be appropriate; a critical requirement in such instances is that the various authors address common issues and that the contribution arising from the set as a whole be both unique and substantial. In essence, irrespective of how it may be framed, any work that contributes significant data and/or extends developmental thinking will be taken under editorial consideration.

Submissions should contain a minimum of 80 manuscript pages (including tables and references); the upper limit of 150–175 pages is much more flexible (please submit four copies; a copy of every submission and associated correspondence is deposited eventually in the archives of the SRCD). Neither membership in the Society for Research in Child Development nor affiliation with the academic discipline of psychology are relevant; the significance of the work in extending developmental theory and in contributing new empirical information is by far the most crucial consideration. Because the aim of the series is not only to advance knowledge on specialized topics but also to enhance cross-fertilization among disciplines or subfields, it is important that the links between the specific issues under study and larger questions relating to developmental processes emerge as clearly to the general reader as to specialists on the given topic.

Potential authors who may be unsure whether the manuscript they are planning would make an appropriate submission are invited to draft an outline of what they propose and send it to the Editor for assessment. This mechanism, as well as a more detailed description of all editorial policies, evaluation processes, and format requirements, is given in the "Guidelines for the Preparation of *Monographs* Submissions," which can be obtained by writing to the Editor designate, Rachel K. Clifton, Department of Psychology, University of Massachusetts, Amherst, MA 01003.